The Court and Character of King James, Written and Taken by Sir A.W. Repr - Primary Source Edition

Anthony Weldon

Nabu Public Domain Reprints:

You are holding a reproduction of an original work published before 1923 that is in the public domain in the United States of America, and possibly other countries. You may freely copy and distribute this work as no entity (individual or corporate) has a copyright on the body of the work. This book may contain prior copyright references, and library stamps (as most of these works were scanned from library copies). These have been scanned and retained as part of the historical artifact.

This book may have occasional imperfections such as missing or blurred pages, poor pictures, errant marks, etc. that were either part of the original artifact, or were introduced by the scanning process. We believe this work is culturally important, and despite the imperfections, have elected to bring it back into print as part of our continuing commitment to the preservation of printed works worldwide. We appreciate your understanding of the imperfections in the preservation process, and hope you enjoy this valuable book.

THE
COURT AND CHARACTER
OF
KING JAMES,

WRITTEN AND TAKEN

By Sir A. W.

BEING AN EYE, AND EARE WITNESSE.

QUI NESCIT DISSIMULARE, NESCIT REGNARE.

LONDON:

Printed by R. J. and are to be sold by John Wright, at the King's Head in the *Old Baily.*

M.DC.L.

Reprinted by G. Smeeton, St. Martin's Church Yard, Charing Cross.

1817.

HOWLETT AND BRIMMER, PRINTERS,
FRITH STREET, SOHO.

THE PUBLISHER TO THE READER.

AMONGST the many remarkable passages in this short relation, the Reader may take notice of five things here discovered.

First, how Almighty God was mockt, and the world abused, by Tuesday Sermons at Court, and the Anniversary Festivals upon the fifth of August, in commemmoration of King James's deliverance from the Gowrie's conspiracy; whereas indeed, there was no such matter, but a mere feigned thing, as appears by the story.

Secondly, how this kingdom was gulled in the supposed treason of Sir Walter Rawley and others, who suffered as Traytors; whereas, to this day, it could never be knowne that ever there was any such treason; but a mere trick of State to remove some bloches out of the way.

Thirdly, the fearful imprecation made by King James against himselfe and his posterity, in the presence of many of his servants, and the Judges, even upon his knees, if he would spare any that were found guilty in the poysoning businesse of Sir Thomas Overbury; but how he failed this story will tell you; and how the justice of God hath been and is upon himselfe and posterity, his owne death, by poyson, and the sufferings of his posterity, doe sufficiently manifest.

Fourthly, the untimely death of that hopeful Prince Henry is here partly discovered; if the Reader cannot in this discourse spell by what hand hee was taken away, yet may he observe a strange connivance at, and contentednesse with the thing done.

Fiftly, here we may see what a slave King James was to his Favourites; this appears by many passages of this story, but especially, by his passion at Greenwich, when the Lieutenant of the Tower told him of Somersets threatening speeches, and by his agony, till he heard that Somerset took his arraignment patiently, and had told no tales.

The summa totalis *of all that I commend from this discourse to the Reader, is, that he would give glory to God, in acknowledging his justice, in ruining that family, by which the eyes of his glory have been so much provoked; the foundation whereof was laid in the Father's reigne, and finished in the Sons; and hereby we may clearly see the truth of God's word, when he said;* They that honour me I will honour them, but they that despise me shall be lightly esteemed.

Lastly, I take the boldnesse to advise all that are faithfull in the Land to take heed how they side with this bloody house, lest they be found opposers of God's purpose, which doubtlesse is, to lay aside that family, and to make it an example to posterity; according to the several imprecations both of King James *and King* Charles.

THE
COURT of KING JAMES;

OR

A general Discourse of some secret passages in State,
Since the Death of that ever-glorious Queen Elizabeth,
Until this present.

By the Authors own observation, who was either an eye,
or eare witness, or from such as were actors in them,
from their own relation.

UPON the twenty-fourth of *March*, 1602, did set the most glorious Sun that ever shined in our Firmament of *England*, (the never to be forgotten Queen *Elizabeth*, of happy memory) about three in the morning, at her Manour of *Richmond*, not only to the inspeakable grief of her Servants in particular, but all her Subjects in general.

And although many of her Courtiers adored that rising Sun, appearing in the North, yet since (not without regret) of their monstrous ingratitude to that Sun now set, and in peace.

No sooner was that Sun set, but Sir *Robert Carew* (her near Kinsman, and whose Family, and himself, she had raised from the degree of a mean Gentleman, to high honor, in title and place) most ingratefully did catch at her last breath, to carry it to the rising Sun then in *Scotland*, notwithstanding a strict charge laid to keep fast all the Gates, yet, his Father being Lord Chamberlaine, he by that means found favour to get out, to carry the first news; which although it obtained for him the Governourship of the Duke of *York*, yet hath set so wide a mark of ingratitude on him, that it will remain to posterity a greater blot, than the honour he obtained afterward, will ever wipe out.

About nine in the morning of that day, was proclaimed King *James* of blessed memory, by the name of *James* the first; and now nothing on all hands, but preparations for accommodating him in his journey for *England*, many posting into *Scotland* for preferment, either by indearing themselves by some merit of their own to the King, or by purchasing friends with their purses, (Gold and Silver being a precious commodity in that Climate, and would procure any thing) and did procure Suits, Honours, and Offices to any that first came; of all which the King afterward extended his bounty, in so large and ample a manner, as procured his own impoverishment, to the pressure of his Subjects, so far as set some distance between him and them, which his wisdom, and Kings craft, could easily at all times reconcile.

The first that came from the King to the Lords in *England*, to give order for all things necessary for the expediting his journey towards *England*, was Sir *Roger Aston*, an *English man* born, but had his breeding wholly in *Scotland*, and had served the King many years as his Barber, an honest and free-hearted man, and of an ancient Family in *Cheshire*, but of no breeding answerable to his birth; yet he was the only man ever employed, as a Messenger from the King to Q. *Elizabeth*, as a Letter carrier only, which expressed their own intentions without any help from him, besides the delivery, but even in that capacity was in very good esteem with her Majesty, and received very royal rewards, which did inrich him, and gave him a better Revenue then most Gentlemen in *Scotland;* for the Queen did find him as faithful to her as to his Master, in which he shewed much wisdom, though of no breeding. In this his imployment I must not pass over one pretty passage, I have heard himself relate; That he did never come to deliver any Letters from his Master, but ever he was placed in the Lobby; the Hangings being turned him, where he might see the Queen dancing to a little Fiddle, which was to no other end, then that he should tell his Master, by her youthful disposition, how likely he was to come to the possession of the Crown he so much thirsted after; for you must understand, the wisest in that Kingdom did believe the King should never enjoy this Crown, as long as there was an old Wife in *England*, which they did believe we ever set up, as the other was dead.

Sir *Roger Aston* presenting himself before the Councel, being but a plain untutored man, being asked how he did, and courted by all the Lords, lighted upon this happy reply; even my Lords, like a poor man, wandring above forty years in a Wilderness, and barren Soyl, am now arrived at the Land of Promise. This man was afterward made Gentleman of the Bed-chamber, Master of the Wardrobe, and invested with such Honours and Offices as he was capable of, and that enabled him to live in a noble way, during his life, and to leave his Daughters great Fortunes; but had you seen how the Lords did vye courtesies to this poor Gentleman, striving who should ingross that Commodity by the largest bounty; you could not but have condemned them of much baseness, especially, seeing when at this time, Offices, and great places of Honor will not be accepted from that Son, the Barber of whose Father was so much courted, but to speak a good word in their behalfs; surely the times are much altered.

And now all preparation was made to meet the King in *Yorke*, that he might in that Northern Metropolis appear like a King of *England*, and take that State on him there, which was not known in *Scotland*. There met him all the Lords of the Councel, and there did they all make Court to the *Scotch-men* that were most in favor with the King, and there did the *Scotch* Courtiers lay the first foundation of their *English* Fortunes; the chief of them was Sir *George Hewme*, a kind of Favourite, but not such as after appeared with young Faces, and smooth Chins, but one that for his wisdom and gravity, had been in some secret Councels with his Master, which created that dearness between them; and the chief of those secrets was that of *Gowries* Conspiracy, though that Nation gave little credit to the Story, but would speak both slightly and despitefully of it, and those of the wisest of that Nation; yet there was a weekly commemoration by the Tuesday Sermon, and an anniversary Feast as great as it was possible, for the preservation, ever on the fifth of *August*, upon which day as Sir *John Ramsey*, after Earl of *Holdernes*, for his good service in that preservation, was the principal Guest, so did the King grant him any Boon he would ask that day; but had such limitations set to his asking, as made his Suit as unprofitable unto him, as that he asked it for, was unserviceable to the King, and indeed did make the *English* believe as little the truth of that Story, as the *Scots* themselves did, and yet on my conscience the good Gentleman did in that as a Lyer often doth, by telling a Lye often believeth it to be a very truth; but the truth was, (although he was not a man capable of much himself) yet had it been true, there was too little done for him, being not true too much; for being an Earl he was in very little esteem, either with his Master, or with the better sort of Courtiers. And I pray God that the effects of those Sermons in the Fathers time for that service, cause no ill effects, or be not one cause of Gods anger with us in the Sons reign.

This Sir *George Hewme* being the only man that was the Guider of the King, and his affairs, all the wiser sort of *English* made their addresses unto him, amongst those Sir *Robert Cecil*, a very wise man, but much hated in *England*, by reason of the fresh bleeding of that universally beloved Earl of *Essex*, and for that was clouded also in the Kings favour; he came to *York*, but lay close, unseen, or scarce known to be in the City, until he knew what entertainment he should receive from the King; for he was in his own, and all mens opinions, so under the Hatches, as not ever to appear above board again (nor did any of the Counter-faction to *Essex*, besides himself, ever attaine to the Kings favour;) but those friends raised by his wit, and purse, did so co-operate (of which Sir *Roger Aston*, that plain man was principal, for which he lost not his labour) that Sir *George Hewme*, and Sir *Robert Cecil* had many secret meetings, did so comply to the admiration of all, did appear, and come out of his Chamber like a Giant, to run his race, for Honor, and Fortune; and who in such dearness, and privacy with the King, as Sir *Robert Cecil*: as if he had been his faithful Servant many years before; yet did not either his Friends, wit or wealth, raise him so much (as some believe) as the ill offices done by him to this Nation, in discovering the nature of the people, and shewing the King the way, how to enhance his Prerogative so above the Laws, that he might inslave the Nation, which though it took well then, yet it hath been of sad and dangerous consequences in after times; for first, he caused a whole Cart-load of Parliament Presidents, that spake the Subjects liberty, to be burnt; next, raising two hundred thousand pound for making two hundred Baronets, telling the King, he should find his *English* Subjects like Asses, on whom he might lay any burthen, and should neither Bit nor Bridle, but their Asses ears; and when the King said, It would discontent the generality of the Gentry, he replyed; Tush, Sir, you want the money, that will do you good, the honor will do them very little; and by these courses he raised himself, friends, and family, to Offices, Honors, and great Possessions, yet as a punishment, he lived long enough to have lost all, had not death prevented him between the *Bath*, and *London*; for the Duke of *Bullion* being then here, about the overture of that unfortunate Match between the Palsgrave, and the Lady *Elizabeth*, had so done his errand, and discovered his jugling; it is most certain, he had been stript of all at his return, which he well understanding from his friends at Court, did expedite his end; but he dyed opportunely to save his honor, and estate, for his Posterity, though to leave a mark of ignominy on himself by that *Herodian* disease, that for all his great Honors, and Possessions, and stately Houses, he found no place but the top of a Mole-hill, near *Maleborough* to end his miserable life; so that it may be said of him, and truly, he dyed of a most loathsome Disease, without house, without pity, without the favour of that Master that had raised him to so high an estate; and yet must he have that right done him (which is also a note of the misfortune of our times) there hath not been any since his time that equalled him to fulfil the Proverb, *Seldom comes a better*; he had great parts, was very wise, full of honour, and bounty, a great lover and rewarder of Virtue, and able parts in others, so they did not aspire too high in places, or look too narrowly into his actions.

The next came on the public Theatre in favour, was *Henry Howard*, a younger Son of the Duke of *Norfolk*, and Lord *Thomas Howard*, the one after Earl of *Northampton*, the other Earl of *Suffolk*, Lord Chamberlain, and after Lord Treasurer, who by *Salisburies* greatness with that Family, rather then by any merit, or wisdom in themselves, raised many great Families of his Children; *Northampton* though a great Clerk, yet not a wise man, but the grossest Flatterer of the World, and as *Salisbury* by his Wit, so this by his Flattery, raised himself; yet one great motive to the raising of that Name of *Howards* was, the Duke of *Norfolk*, suffering for the Queen of *Scots*, the Kings Mother, yet did *Suffolk* so far forget the start of *Northampton*, that *Northampton* never after loved him but from teeth outwards, only had so much discretion as not to fall to actual enmity, to the overthrow of both, and the weakning their faction; *Suffolk* also using him with all submissive respect, not for any love but hope of gaining his great estate, and sharing it amongst his Children; *Northamptons* distaste was such, by his loss of the Treasurers place, which he had with such assurance promised to himself in his thoughts, that except what he gave to Master *Henry Howard*, the rest he gave to the Earl of *Arundel*, who by his observance, but more especially by giving *Northampton* all his Estate if he never returned from travel, had wrought himself so far into his affection, that he doted on him.

And now the principal managers of the *English* affairs were *Salisbury, Suffolk, Northampton, Buckhurst, Egerton*, Lord Keeper, *Worcester*, and the old Admiral for the *Scots*, Sir *George Hewme*, now Earl of *Dunbar*, Secretary *Elfeston*, after Earl of *Balmerino*, and as wise a man as was in *England*, or *Scotland*, the Lord of *Kinlosse*, a very honest, but weak man.

You are now to observe, that *Salisbury* had shaken off all that were great with him, and of his Faction in Queen *Elizabeths* day, as Sir *Walter Rawleigh*, Sir *George Carew*, the Lord *Grey*, the Lord *Cobham*: the three first, very able men as the World had, the last but one degree from a fool, yet served their turns better then a wiser man, by his greatness with the Queen, for they would put him on any thing, and make him tell any Lye, with as great confidence as a truth. Three of these were utterly ruined, as you shall hear in the following Discourse, the fourth being a very wise man, contented himself with a mean place, that was worthy of a much greater; and although very active formerly, called to mind this saying: *Fœlix quem faciunt, &c.* and medled with no State business, his wisdom foretelling his Fate, if he had done otherwise; for he did see one better head-piece then his own, sit tottering at that time, and fell off afterwards, which made him think it was good sleeping in a whole skin.

The King no sooner came to *London*, but notice was taken of a rising Favourite, the first Meteor of that nature appearing in our climate; as the King cast his eye upon him for affection, so did all the Courtiers, to adore him, his name was Mr. *James Hay*,* a Gentleman that long lived in *France*, and some say, of the *Scottish* Guard to that King; this Gentleman coming over to meet the King, and share with him in his new Conquest (according to the *Scottish* phrase) it should seem had some former acquaintance with the then Leiger Embassadour in *Scotland* for the *French* King, who coming with His Majesty into *England*, presented this Gentleman, as a well accomplished Gentleman, to the King, in such an high commendation as engendred such a liking as produced a Favourite; in thankful acknowledgement whereof, he did him many fair offices for the present, and coming afterwards an extraordinary Embassador to our King, made him the most sumptuous Feast at *Essex* house, that ever was seen before, never equalled since, in which was such plenty, and Fish of that immensity, brought out of *Muscovia*, that Dishes were made to contain them (no

---

* This extravagant man in one of his pompous entrées into Paris, had his horse's shoes made of silver. King James created him Lord Hay. His next title was that of Viscount Doncaster, and then Earl Carlisle. His love of dress was so great, that it continued to the last moment of his life, when he knew he was given over by his Physicians; abstracting him from his vanity, Wilson says he was a complete gentleman, and of great bounty. He died October 25, 1630.

Dishes in all *England* before could ne're hold them) and after that a costly Voydee, and after that a Mask, of choyse Noble-men, and Gentlemen, and after that a most costly and magnificent Banquet, the King, Lords, and all the prime Gentlemen then about *London* being invited thither. Truly, he was a most compleat, and well accomplished Gentleman, modest, and Court-like, and of so fair a demeanor, as made him be generally beloved; and for his wisdom, I shall give you but one character for all: He was ever great with all the Favourites of his time, and although the King did often change, yet he was *(semper eidem)* with the King, and Favourites, and got by both; for although Favourites had that exorbitant power over the King, to make him grace and disgrace whom they pleased, he was out of that power, and the only exception to that general rule; and for his gettings, it was more then almost all the Favourites of his time, which appeared in those vast expences of all sorts, and had not the bounty of his mind exceeded his gettings, he might have left the greatest estate that ever our age or climate had heard of; he was indeed made for a Courtier, who wholly studied his Master, and understood him better then any other.

He was imployed in very many of the most weighty affairs, and sent with the most stately Embassies of our times, which he performed with that wisdom, and magnificency, that he seemed an honor to his King and Country, for his carriage in State affairs; he was termed by some Princes the Kings Juggler, he married the Daughter and Heir of the Lord *Denny*, after the Earl of *Northumberlands* Daughter, and was hated of none that ever I heard of, but the Earl of *Northampton*,* who had no patience to see him, being himself of so venemous and cankred a disposition that indeed he hated all men of noble parts, nor loved any but flatterers, like himself; yet it was a greater question, whether he hated the Earl of *Carlile*, or Sir *Robert Mansel* most; by whom he hath been heard to say; *Body of God, I will be content to be damned perpetually in Hell, to be revenged of that proud Welsh-man;* and did so hate him, that he kept an Inquisition on him seven years, to prove that he had couzened the King of fourteen thousand pound, which at seven years end at an hearing before the King, the Lords,

---

* Northampton built many Alms-houses, he also erected Suffolk-house, at Charing Cross, now called Northumberland House. In the Aulicus Coquinariæ, it says, he built that handsome Covent at Greenwich, for decayad Ladies and Gentlemen. He was a lover of reading; and died a Bachelor, in 1613, leaving the whole of his fortune to his two Nephews, the Earl of Suffolk and the Earl of Arundel.

the Queen, and all the Ladies being present, with all the gallantry of the Court, ended in one pair of silk Stockins, given by one for a New-years Gift to Master *Wels*, Sir *Robert Mansels* Servant; at which, the King stood up, and sware very deeply; *Do you believe I will take a pair of silk Stockins for my fourteen thousand pound, give me that; is this all the fruit of seven years Commission?* which words, Sir *Robert Mansel* kneeled down, and said, *I will now, Sir, take all the faults they can charge my servant with upon myself*; at which the King was very angry, that so noble a Gentleman, who had so well acquitted himself, and Honour, should intrust it in the keeping of a Servant; at the end of all the Earl of *Salisbury* kneeled down, and said; *Sir, if you will suffer malice so far to prevail, as to have your honest Servants traduced, to satisfie the humours of any: I beseech you take my staffe, for were myself, and the Earl of* Worcester *here present, put in the ballance against Sir* Robert Mansel, *we should prove too light; I am in a great Place, and cannot say, but by my self I may fail, yet not with our own wills; therefore Sir, if you will suffer such inquisitions, there will be no serving your Majesty, in such places as I hold, by your Majesties favor.* Thus ended the Earl of *Northamptons* malice, which only served to honor Sir *Robert Mansel*, and make a scorn of himself, and this only to make the venom of this Monster appear, who did flatter the King, and dissemble with God.

And now begins Embassadors to appear from divers Princes, the Prime was *Roney* Duke of *Sullia*, from the *French* King, the Constable of *Castile* from the *Spanish* King, the Count of *Arremberg* from the Arch Duke; the former come to congratulate only, and desired the confirmation of the ancient amity betwixt the two Crowns, the latter two about the establishing a firm Peace betwixt these two Kingdoms, that had lived in perpetual war, and hatred of each other, by which it might appear where the advantage of such a peace might fail, by those that sought, or rather bought it with an infinite mass of treasure, prodigally cast about the *English* Court.

To bring these Embassadors over, were appointed Sir *Robert Mansel*, Vice-Admiral of the narrow Seas, and Sir *Jerome Turner* his Vice-Admiral; the first commanded to attend at *Graveling* for the *Spanish* Embassador, the latter at *Calis* for the *French*; but the *French* coming first, and hearing the Vice-Admiral was to attend him, the Admiral the other; in a scorn put himself in a Passage boat of *Calis*, came forth with flag in top; instantly Sir *Jerome Turner* sent to know of the Admiral what he should do; Sir *Robert Mansel* sent him word, to shoot, and strike him, if he would not take in the flag; this, as it made the flag be pulled in, so a great complaint, and 'twas believed it would have undone Sir *Robert Mansel*, the *French* faction put it so home, but he maintained the act, and was the better beloved of his Master ever after, to his dying day.

This makes it appear how jealous old Commanders were of their honor, the King, and Kingdoms, which since hath been so prodigally wasted, as we are utterly bankrupt, having spent our old Stock, and not bravery enough to erect a new.

The Constable of *Castile* so plyed his Masters business (in which he spared for no cost) that he procured a peace so advantagious for *Spaine*, and so disadvantagious for *England*, that it and all Christendom have since both seen and felt the lamentable effect thereof, there was not one Courtier of note, that tasted not of *Spains* bounty, either in Gold, or Jewels, and among them, not any in so large a proportion as the Countess of *Suffolke*, who shared in her Lords interest, being then a potent man, and in that interest which she had, in being Mistris to that little great Secretary (little in body and stature, but great in wit and policy) the sole manager of State affairs, so it may be said, she was a double sharer, and in truth *Audley end*, that famous and great structure, had its foundation of *Spanish* Gold.

The King was a peaceable and merciful Prince (yet God for some secret intent best known to himself) laid the foundation of his reign, with the greatest mortality ever before heard of in this Kingdom, by a fearful plague, and some by that, judged what his future reign would be, yet their wisdoms failed, for he was a King of mercy as well as peace, never cruel, yet surely it had some moral.

He was forced by that contagion to leave the Metropolis, and goe into a buy corner in *Wiltshire*, *Wilton* the Earl of *Pembrokes* House, in which time of his abode there, a kind of Treason brake forth, but what it was, as no man could then tell, so it is left with so dark a Comment, that posterity will never understand the Text, or remember any such treason, it is true, some lost their lives, yet the world was never satisfied of the justice, and one of them, (and that the only mark of Tyranny of this good Kings reign) executed many years after without all president, and on my conscience without any just cause, and even against that good Kings will, who in many things was over-awed by his timerous disposition.

But the *Spanish* faction, and *Spanish* Gold betrayed his life, as they had done the Kingdoms before, and I believe it was one of the greatest Master peeces of that Embassador, to purchase *Rawleighs* head, yet had not *Bristol* cooperated, the King would never have consented, and it may be he had his secret ends, fearing his wisdom might once again have raised him, to have looked over *Sherborne* Castle, once his own, and how unjustly taken from him God will one day judge; I know not whether there be a curse on those that are owners of it, as Fables report, but I am confident there is a curse on *Bristol* for taking away his life; I will not take upon me too far to pry into Gods Arke, yet what is like to befal him, and hath already, his son (as hopeful a Gentleman as any in the Kingdom) may give some token of Gods anger against him and his Family.

But because I will not leave you altogether blinde-folded, I shall as near as I can lead you to the discovery of this Treason, which consisted of Protestants, Puritants, Papists, and Atheists: a strange medley you will say, to meet in one and the same Treason, and keep counsel, which surely they did, because they knew not of any; the Protestants were the Lord *Cobham*, and *George Brook* his Brother, the one very learned and wise, the other a most silly Lord, the Puritan the Lord *Grey* of *Wilton*, a very hopeful Gentleman, blasted in the very Bud; the Papists *Watson*, and *Clarke* Priests; and *Parham* a Gentleman, the Atheist Sir *Walter Rawleigh* then generally so believed, though after brought by affliction (the best School Mistris) to be, and so dyed, a most religious Gentleman. This treason was compounded of most strange ingredients, (and more strange then true) it was very true, most of these were discontented, to see *Salisbury* their old friend so high, to trample on them, that before had been his chief supporters (and being ever of his faction) now neglected and contemned; it was then believed an errend trick of State to overthrow some, and disable others, knowing their strong abilities might otherwise live to overthrow *Salisbury*, for they were intimate in all his secret Councels for the ruine of *Essex*, especially *Rawleigh*, *Grey*, and *Cobham*; though the latter was a fool, yet had been very useful to them (as the Toole in the hand of the Work-man,) to have singled out these without some Priests, which were Traytors by the Law, had smelt too rank, and appeared too poor and plaine a trick of State; and *Salisbury* in this had a double benefit: First, in ridding himself of such as he feared would have been thornes in his sides. Secondly, by endearing himself to the King, by shewing his diligence, and vigilancy for his safety, so that it might be said of him as of *Cæsar* in another case (*Inveniam aut faciam*) I will either find out a Treason or make one, and this had been a pretty trick had it been only to disgrace, without taking away Life; but how this peece of policy may stand with Religion, I fear by this time he too well understands; and this Plot as near as I can tell you (and I dare say my intelligence gave me as near a guess as ever any man had) was, that all these in a discontented humour had by *Watson*, and *Clark*, being Confessors, dealt with Count *Aremberge*, the Arch Dukes Embassador, to negotiate with the Arch Duke to raise an Army, and invade *England*, and they would raise another of Papists, and Male-contents to joyn, for you must understand the King was believed an errand Puritan, (*Cujus contrarium verum est*) how likely this Plot was, let the world judge, that the King of *Spaine*, who had bought peace at so dear a rate, and found it so advantagious to him, by the lamentable experience he had formerly in the wars with this formidable state, should seek to break it so soon; and had it been a real Treason, the state had been bound to have rewarded these Traytors, as the best piece of service done in *England* all that Kings reign (it was indeed those that made the Peace, not those that endeavoured the breaking of it, were the Traytors, and are to be cursed by all Posterity) yet this foolish Plot served well enough to take some blocks out of the way, that might afterwards have made some of them stumble, to the breaking of their own necks.

They were all Arraigned of Treason at *Winchester*, whither the King sent some secretly to observe all passages, upon whose true and faithful relations of the innocency of the Persons Arraigned, and slight proof upon which they were condemned, he would not be drawn to sign any Warrant for the execution of *Rawleigh*, *Cobham*, and *Grey*, very hardly for any of the rest, the two Priests excepted.

For *Rawleighs* defence, it was so brave and just, as (had he not wilfully cast himself, out of very weariness, as unwilling to detain the Company longer) no Jury could ever have cast him; all the Evidence brought against him was *Cobhams* Accusation, which he only desired might appear (*viva voce*) and he would yield without further defence, but that they knew full well *Cobham* would not, nor could not accuse him, having been tampered with by *Wade*, then Lieutenant of the Tower, and *Salisburies* great Creature; *Wade* desired it under his hand, that also he refused, at last *Wade* got a trick by his cunning, to surprize *Cobhams* weakness, to get him write his name to a Blank, to which *Wade*, no question, wrote the accusation, as will appear hereafter; for *Salisbury* urging *Rawleigh* often, if *Cobham* had accused him under his hand would he then yield; *Rawleigh* replyed, He knew *Cobham* weak of Judgement, and did not know how that weakness might be wrought upon, but was confident he would not to his face accuse him, and therefore would not put his fortune and all on that; at which fence he stood till nine at night: at least his fate carried him against his reason, and he yielded upon the producing his hand, which was instantly pulled out (and was in truth his hand) but not his act, or deed; so at that present was *George Brooke*, *Watson*, and *Clarke* executed, *Parham* acquitted, and Sir *Walter Rawleigh* executed many years after for the same treason, as much against all reason, as all, or any president; yea after he had been a General by the Kings Commission, and had by that, power of the Lives of many others, utterly against the Civil Law, which saith, *He that hath power of the Lives of others, ought to be Master of his own.* But the *Spaniard* was so powerful at that time at Court, as that Faction could command the Life of any man that might prove dangerous to their designs; *Grey* and *Cobham* dyed in their restraint, the one much pitied, the other scorned, and his death as base, for he dyed lousie for want of Apparel, and Linnen; and had starved, had not a Trencher-scraper some time his Servant in Court relieved him with scraps, in whose house he dyed, being so poor a house as he was forced to creep up a Ladder into a little hole to his Chamber; which was a strange judgement, and unpresidented, that a man of seven thousand pound *per annum*, and of a personal estate of thirty thousand pounds (of all which the King was cheated, of what should Escheated to him, that he could not give him any maintenance, as in all cases the King doth, unless out of his own Revenue of the Crown, which was the occasion of this Lords want, (his Wife being very rich, would not give him the crums that fell from her table;) and this was a just judgment of God on him; and now, because it will be pertinent in this place to let you understand, that *Rawleigh* had his Life surreptiously taken away, I shall give you a true story.

Queene *Anne*, that brave Princess, was in a desperate, and believed, incurable Disease, whereof the Physitians were at the furthest end of their studies to find the cause, at a *Non-plus* for the Cure, Sir *Walter Rawleigh*, being by his long studies an admirable Chymist, undertook, and performed the Cure, for which he would receive no other reward, but that her Majesty would procure that certain Lords might be sent to examin *Cobham*, whether he had accused Sir *Walter Rawleigh* of Treason at any time under his hand; the King at the

Queens request (and in Justice could do no less) sends six Lords, which I take were, the Duke of *Leonox, Salisbury, Worcester, Suffolk,* Sir *George Carew,* and Sir *Julius Cæsar,** to demand of *Cobham,* whether he had not under his hand accused Sir *Walter Rawleigh* at *Winchester,* upon that Treason he was Arraigned for; *Cobham* did protest never, nor could he, but said he, That Villain *Wade* did often solicite me, and not prevailing, got me by a trick to write my name upon a piece of white Paper, which I thinking nothing, did, so that if any Charge came under my hand, it was forged by that Villain *Wade,* by writing something above my hand without my consent or knowledge. These six returning to the King, made *Salisbury* their Spokes-man, who said, Sir, my L. *Cobham* hath made good all that ever he wrote, or said, and this was an equivocating trick, for it was true, he made good what ever he writ, but never wrote any thing to accuse *Rawleigh;* by which you see the baseness of these Lords, the credulity of the King, and the ruin of Sir *Walter Rawleigh.* I appeal now to the judgement of all the world, whether these six Lords were not the immediate Murtherers, and no question, shall be called to a sad account for it.

And thus have you a true relation of the Treason, and Traytors, with all the windings and turnings in it, and all passages appertaining to it; and by it, you may see the slavery these great men were inslaved in by *Salisbury,* none durst testifie such a truth, as the not testifying, lost their most precious Souls.

And now doth the King return to *Windsor,* where there was an apparition of *Southamptons* being a Favourite to his Majesty, by that privacy and dearness presented to the Court view, but *Salisbury* liking not that any of *Essex* his faction should come into play, made that apparition appear as it were in *transitu,* and so vanished, by putting some jealousie, that he did not much desire to be in his Queens company, yet love and regality must admit of no partnership.

Then was there in requital of the *Spanish* Embassadors, two stately Embassies addressed, the one to *Spaine,* the other to the Arch Duke, to have that peace they so dearly purchased confirmed, and sworn to by ours, as formerly by them; the old Lord Admiral was sent to *Spain,* the Earl of *Hartford* for *Bruxels,* that the Duke of *Leonox* might have the better opportunity. The *Spaniard* was astonished at the

---

* Sir Julius Cæsar died April 28, 1630, and is buried in Great St. Helen's Church, near Bishopsgate, London.

braveness of our Embassie, and the handsome Gentlemen (in both which, few Embassies ever equalled this) for you must understand the Jesuits reported our Nation to be ugly, and like Devils, as a punishment sent to our Nation for casting off the Popes supremacy; and they pictured Sir *Francis Drake* generally half a Man, half a Dragon. When they beheld them after the Shape of Angels, they could not well tell whether to trust their own eyes, or their Confessors reports, yet they then appeared to them, as to all the world, monstrous Lyers.

The Embassador had his reception with as much state, as his entertainment with bounty, the King defraying all charges, and they were detained at their Landing longer than ordinary, to have provisions prepared in their passage to *Madrid*, with all the bounty was possible, to make the whole country appear a Land of *Canaan*, which was in truth, but a Wilderness.

In their abode there, although they gave them Rost-meat, yet they beat them with the spits, by reporting that the *English* did steal all the Plate, when in truth it was themselves, who thought to make Hay while the Sun shined, not thinking ever more to come to such a Feast, to fill their purses as well as their bellies, (for food and coyn, are equally alike scarce with that Nation) this report passed for currant, to the infinite dishonour of our Nation, there being at that time the prime gallantry of our Nation.

Sir *Robert Mansell*, who was a man born to vindicate the honour of his Nation as his own, being Vice-Admiral, and a man on whom the old Admiral wholly relyed, having dispatched the ships to be gone the next morning, came in very late to supper; Sir *Richard Levison* sitting at the upper end of the table among the Grandees, the Admiral himself not supping that night, being upon the dispatch of Letters, the table upon Sir *Robert Mansels* entrance offered to rise, to give him place, but he sate down instantly at the lower end, and would not let any man stir, and falling to his meat, did espy a *Spaniard*, as the Dishes emptied, ever putting some in his bosome, some in his breeches, that they both strutted, Sir *Robert Mansel* sent a Message to the upper end of the table to Sir *Richard Levison*, to be delivered in his eare, that whatsoever he saw him do, he should desire the Gentlemen and Grandees to sit quiet, for there should be no cause of any disquiet; on the sudden Sir *Robert Mansel* steps up, takes this *Spaniard* in his armes, at which the table began to rise; Sir *Richard Levison* quiets them, brings him up to the end amongst the Grandees, then pulls out the Plate from his bosome, breeches, and every part about him, which did so amase the *Spaniard*, and vindicate that aspersion cast on our Nation, that never after was there any such sillable heard, but all honour done to the Nation, and all thanks to him in particular.

From thence, next day they went for *Madrid*, where all the royal entertainment *Spaine* could yield was given them, and at the end of the Grand entertainment and Revels, which held most part of the night; as they were all returning to their Lodgings, the street being made light by white Wax lights, and the very night forced into a day, by shining light, as they were passing in the street, a *Spaniard* catcheth off Sir *Robert Mansels* hat, with a very rich jewel in it, and away he flies; Sir *Robert* not being of a spirit to have any thing violently taken from him, nor of such a Court-like complement, to part with a jewel of that price, to one no better acquainted with him, hurls open the Boot, follows after the fellow, and some three Gentlemen did follow him, to secure him, houseth the Fellow in the house of an Algnarel, which is a great Officer, or Judge in *Spaine*; this Officer wondring at the manner of their coming, the one with his hat, and sword in his hand, the other with all their swords; Demands the cause, They tell him; he saith, surely none can think his house a Sanctuary, who is to punish such offenders; but Sir *Robert Mansel* would not be so put off with the *Spaniards* gravity, but enters the house, leaving two at the Gate, to see that none should come out, while he searched, a long time they could find nothing, and the Algnarel urging this as an affront, at last, looking down into a Well of a small depth, he saw the fellow stand up to the neck in water; Sir *Robert Mansel* seized on his hat, and jewel, leaving the fellow to the Algnarel, but he had much rather have fingered the jewel, and his gravity told Sir *Robert Mansel*, he could not have it without form of Law, which Sir *Robert* dispensed with, carrying away his hat, and jewel, and never heard further of the business; now the truth was, the fellow knew his Burrough well enough, as well as some Thieves of our Nation, after they have done a Robbery, would put themselves into a prison of their acquaintance, assuring themselves none would search there; or rather as our Recorders of *London*, whose chief revenue, for themselves, and servants, is from Thieves, Whores, and Bawds, therefore this Story cannot seem strange in *England*.

The other Embassador sent to the Arch Duke was, the old Earl of *Hertford*, who was conveyed over by one of the Kings Ships, by Sir *William Monson*, in whose passage a *Dutch* Man of War coming by that Ship, would not vail, as the manner is, acknowledging by that, our Soveraignty over the Sea, Sir *William Monson* gave him a shot to instruct him manners, but instead of hearing, he taught him by returning another, he acknowledged no such Soveraignity, this was the very first indignity and affront ever offered to the royal ships of *England* which since have been most frequent; Sir *William Monson* desired my Lord of *Hertford* to go into the Hold, and he would instruct him by stripes, that refused to be taught by fair means; but the Earl charged him on his allegiance first to land him, on whom he was appointed to attend; so to his great regret, he was forced to endure that indignity, for which I have often heard him wish he had been hanged, rather then, live that unfortunate Commander of a Kings Ship, to be Chronicled for the first that ever endured that affront, although it was not in his power to have helped it; yet by his favor, it appeared but a copy of his countenance, for it had been but hazarding hanging to have disobeyed my Lords Commandment, and it had been infinite odds he had not been hanged, having to friend him, the House of *Suffolk*; nor would he have been so sensible of it, had he not been of the *Spanish* Faction and that a *Dutch* Ship.

Now did these great Mannagers of the State (of which *Salisbury* was chief) after they had packed the Lords, begin to deal the government of the Kingdom amongst themselves, and perswaded the King to leave the State affairs to them, and to betake himself to some Country recreations, which they found him addicted unto, for the City, and business did not agree with him; to that end purchased, built, and repaired at *New-market*, and *Royston*, and this pleased the Kings humour well, rather that he might enjoy his Favourite with more privacy, then that he loved the sport; then must *Theobalds* be in his own possession, as not fit for a King to be beholding to a subject for an House of daily use, but because the King had so much want of monies to express his love, and bounty to his Native Nation, *Salisbury* would exchange, and made such an advantage, that he sold his House for fifty years purchase, and that so cunningly, as hardly to be discerned, but by a curious sight, for he fleeted off the cream of the Kings Mannors in many Counties, not any two lying in any one County, and made choyce of the most in the remotest Counties, only built his nest at *Hatfield*, within the County where his Father had built his, yet kept he still the house of *Theobalds*, for he and his posterity were to be perpetual Keepers of the House, and Parks adjacent; by this he not only shewed his wisdom for his own benefit, but to the world (what the Kings natural disposition was) to be easily abused, and would take counterfeit Coyn for current payment.

And to fit the Kings humor and dissolve him in that delight he was most addicted to, as well as to serve *Salisburies* own ends, and satisfie his revenge upon some neighbouring Gentlemen, that formerly would not sell him some convenient parcels of Land neighbouring on *Theobalds*, he puts the King on enlarging the Park, walling, and storing it with red Dear; and I dare affirm, with that work he was so well pleased, and did more glory in than his Predecessors did in the conquest of *France;* and as it was most true, so an ill Omen, that the King loved Beasts better then he did men, and took more delight in them, and was more over the life of a Stagg then of a man; yet this was the weakness of his Judgment, and poorness of his spirit, rather than any innate cruelty, for he was not naturally cruel over lives, though in displacing Officers, which naturally he did believe, was as glorious, as to overthrow, and conquer Kings.

But yet for all their setting their Cards, and playing their Games to their own advantages, of getting much for themselves, and friends, there was one Knave in the Pack, would cousen their designs, and Trump in their way, if he might not share with them in their winning; that was one *Lake*, a Clerk of the Signet, after Secretary, and after that turned out in disgrace; and in truth, was only wise in the worlds opinion, could swim being held up by the chin; but at his fall all his weaknesses were discovered, and that the world had been deceived in him, I will instance in one particular, amongst many, that shall give you full assurance; being in disgrace, he gave two thousand pound but to kiss the Kings hand, believing that after that, he might have access as formerly; after he had paid his mony, he was never suffered to see the King more, only jeered at by all the Court for his folly, and went sneaking up and down contemned of all men.

This *Lake* was a Fellow of mean birth, and meaner breeding, being an under Servant to make Fires in Secretary *Walsinghams* Chamber, and there got some experience, which afterwards in the Kings time made him appear an able man, which in the Queens time, when there was none in Court but men of eminences, made him an inconsiderable Fellow; this *Lake* had linked himself in with the *Scottish* Nation, progging for Suits, and helping them to fill their Purses; as they did believe, there was not so able a man in the Kingdom (for in truth ever since Queen *Elizabeths* death, the raising mony hath been the only way to raise men, as being held the essential property of a wise man, to know how to bring in mony *(per fas aut nefas)* and amongst all the

Scots, he wholly applyed himself to those of the Bed-chamber, and of nearest access to His Majesty.

For his good service of abusing his Country, and Country-men, he was made Clerk of the Signet, to wait on the King in his Hunting journies, and in these journies got all the Bills signed, even for the greatest Lords (all Packets being addressed to him) so that even *Salisbury*, and *Northampton*, and the greatest Lords made Court to him; by this means did he raise himself from a mean to a great fortune, but so overawed by his Wife, that if he did not what she commanded, she would beat him, and in truth his wife was afterwards his overthrow; besides, he would tell Tales, and let the King know the passages of Court, and great men, as who was *Salisburies* Mistris, and governed all, who governed *Northampton*, and discovered the Bawdery, which did infinitely please the Kings humour, and in truth had so much craft, as he served his turn upon all, but was engrossed by none but by the Bed-chamber, who stuck so close to him, that they could not yet remove him. And now do the *English* Faction (seeing they could never sever the *Scots* from him) endeavour to raise a mutiny against the *Scots* that were his supporters, their Agents divuldging every where, the *Scots* would get all, and would beggar the Kingdom; the *Scots* on the other side complain to the King, they were so poor, they underwent the by-word of beggarly *Scots*; to which the King returned this answer (as he had a very ready wit) Content yourselves, I will shortly make the English as beggarly as you, and so end that controversie; this is as true as he truly performed it, for however he enriched many in particular, as *Salisbury, Suffolk, Northampton, Worcester, Lake, &c.* yet he did begger himself, and the Nation in general.

This also was inculcated into the ears of the Parliament, when that great business about the union was in debate, which was much crossed by that opinion; if he had already impoverished the Kingdom: by the union, they would bankrupt it. But since you see by their own valour and bravery of spirit, they have made us begg a re-union with them, and for ought we see, all our happiness is derived from their favours.

They that lived at Court, and were curious observers of every man's actions, could have then affirmed, that *Salisbury, Suffolk* and *Northampton*, and their friends did get more then the whole Nation of *Scotland*, (*Dunbar* excepted) for whatever others got, they spent here, only *Dunbar* laid a foundation of a great Family, which did all revert into

England again, with his Daughters marriage with the House of *Suffolk*, so in truth, all the water run to their Mills.

It is most true, that many *Scots* did get much, but not more with one hand, then they spent with the other, witness the Earl of *Kelley*, *Annundale*, &c. nay, that great Getter, the Earl of *Carlisle* also, and some private Gentlemen; as *Gideon Murrey, John Achmoty, James Baily, John Gib,* and *Barnard Lindley,* got some pretty estate, not worthy either the naming or enjoying; old Servants should get some moderate estates to leave to posterity.

But these and all the *Scots* in general, got, scarce the Tythe of those *English* Getters, that can be said did stick by them, or their posterity; besides, *Salisbury* had one trick to get the kernel, and leave the *Scots* but the shell, yet cast all the envy on them; He would make them buy Books of Fee-farms, some one hundred pound *per annum*, some one hundred Marks, and he would compound with them for a thousand pound, which they were willing to embrace, because they were sure to have them pass without any controle, or charge, and one thousand pound appeared to them that never saw ten pound before, an inexhaustible treasure; then would *Salisbury* fill up this Book with such prime Land, as should be worth 10 or 20 thousand pound, which was easie for him, being Treasurer, so to do, and by this means *Salisbury* inriched himself infinitely, yet cast the envy on the *Scots,* in whose names these Books appeared, and are still upon Record to all posterity; though *Salisbury* had the Honey, they poor Gentlemen but part of the Wax; *Dunbar* only had his Agents, and could play his own Game, which they durst not cross; so was the poor King and State cheated on all hands.

And now did a contention arise between the *English* and *Scots,* about the election of a Favourite, out of whether Nation he should come; now was *Montgomery* in the waine, being given more to his own pleasures, then to observe the King, so that alway the Earl of *Carlisle* did invest him in his room; he as soon by his neglective carriage did devest himself, yet was he ever in the Kings good opinion, and one that he put more trust in at that time of his death, then in all his other servants.

Then was a young Gentleman, Master *Robert Carre*, who had his breeding in *France*, and was newly returned from Travail, a Gentleman very handsome, and well bred, and one that was observed to spend his time in serious studies, and did accompany himself with none but men of such eminencies, as by whom he might be bettered; this Gentleman the *Scots* so wrought it, that they got him into a Grooms place of the Bedchamber, and was very well pleasing to all; he did more than any other associate himself, with Sir *Thomas Overbury*, a man of excellent parts, (but those made him proud, over-valuing himself, and under-valuing others, and was infected with a kind of insolency) with this Gentleman spent he most of his time, and drew the eyes of the Court, as well as the affection of his Master upon him, yet very few, but such as were the curious observers, of those times could discern, the drawing of the Kings affection, until upon a Coronation day, riding in with the L. *Dingwell* to the Tilt-yard, his Horse fell with him, and brake his legg, he was instantly carried into Master *Riders* house at *Charing cross*, and the news as instantly carried to the King, having little desire to behold the triumph, but much desired to have it ended, and no sooner ended but the King went instantly to visit him, and after, by his daily visiting, and mourning over him, taking all care for his speedy recovery, made the day-break of his glory appear, every Courtier now concluding him, now actually a favourite.

Lord! how the great men flocked then to see him, and to offer to his Shrine in such abundance, that the King was forced to lay a restraint, least it might retard his recovery by spending his spirits: and to facilitate the cure, care was taken for a choyse Dyet for himself, and Chirurgions, with his Attendants, and no sooner recovered but a proclaimed Favourite.

Then the *English* Lords, who formerly coveted an *English* Favourite (and to that end the Countess of *Suffolk* did look out choyse young men, whom she daily curled, and perfumed their breaths) left all hope, and she her curling and perfuming, all adoring this rising Sun, every man striving to invest himself into this mans favour (not sparing for bounty nor flattery) which was not hard to be obtained, being naturally more adicted to the *English* then to the *Scotch*, in so much that he endeavoured to forget his native Country, and his Fathers house, having none of note about him but *English*, and but one besides *English*, in any familiarity with him, which was Sir *Robert Carre* his Kinsman; but above all was Sir *Thomas Overbury* his *Pythias*, then was the strife between *Salisbury* and *Suffolk*, who should engross him, and make him their Monopoly; each presenting, proffering, and accumulating favors upon *Overburies* kindred, the Father made a Judge in *Wales*, and himself offered an office, but *Overbury*, naturally of an insolent spirit, which was elevated by being so intimate with a favourite, and wholly having ingrossed that commodity, which could not be retayled, but him and his favor; with a kind of scorn neglected their friendships, yet made use of both.

Now was *Carre* Knighted, and made Gentleman of the Bedchamber, and *Overburies* pride rose with the others honors, still storming the Chapman, as they did by their cheap offices undervalue so precious a commodity.

Northampton finding himself neglected by so mean a fellow, cast about another way, and followed *Balaams* councel, by sending a *Moabitish* Woman unto him, in which he made use of *Copinger* a Gentleman, who had spent a fair fortune left by his Ancestors, and now, for maintenance, was forced to lead the life of a Serving man, (that formerly kept many to serve him) and as an addition, the worst of that kind, a flat Bawd.

This Gentleman had lived a scandalous life, by keeping a Whore of his own, which for the honor of her Family I will not name, therefore was fittest to trade in that commodity for another, and in truth was fit to take any impression baseness could stamp on him, as the sequel of this Story will manifest; This *Moabitish* Woman was a Daughter of the Earl of *Suffolk*, married to a young noble gentleman, the Earl of *Essex*.

This Train took, and the first private meetings were at *Copingers* house, and himself Bawd to their Lust, which put him into a far greater bravery for a time, then when he was Master of his own, but it had bitterness on all hands in the end. This privacy in their stollen pleasures, made *Copinger* a friend to *Northampton*, and *Suffolk* though but a Servant to Viscount *Rochester*, for so now was he called, and now had they linked him so close, as no breaking from them.

Overbury was that *John Baptist* that reproved the Lord, for the Sin of using the Lady, and abusing the young Earl of *Essex*; would call her Strumpet, her Mother and Brother Bawds, and used them with so much scorn, as in truth was not to be endured by a fellow of his rank, to persons of that quality, how faulty soever otherwise they were.

Then to satisfie *Overbury*, and blot out the name of Sin, his Love led him into a more desperate way, by a resolution to marry another mans Wife, against this then did *Overbury* bellow lowder, and in it, shewed himself more like an affectionate, then a discreet and moderate friend: had he compounded but one dram of discretion with an ounce of affection, he might with such a receipt, have preserved his own life, and their fortunes and honors.

For those that infinitely hated that family, did has infinitely condemn his insolent carriage, and behaviour towards them; so that had any of those Brothers, or name, killed *Overbury* either by picking a quarrel with him, or Pistolling him, or any other desperate way, or bravely in a Duel, upon some other ground of a quarrel, then blemishing their Sister, the world would have justified the action, however he had stood with God; but *Buchanons* character of that Family, bars all expectation of so much bravery of spirit; but a Counsel must be held, to put him to death by some baser means.

The Plot then must be, he must be sent a Leidger Embassadour into *France*, which by obeying, they should be rid of so great an eye-sore; by disobeying, he incurred the displeasure of his Prince; a contempt, that he could not expect less then imprisonment for, and by that means be sequestered from his friends.

And thus far I do believe the Earl of *Sommerset* (for so was he now created) was consenting; this Stratagem took, and *Overbury* might truly say, *(Video meliora, de tenior a sequor)* for he indeed made the worst choyse, it could not be thought, but such an imployment was far above his desert, and much better for him to have accepted, then to be confined to a loathsome Prison, and for want of judgement, had his suffering been less then loss of Life, he had not been worthy of pity: but, *Jupiter quos vult perdere hos dement at*; he would to the Tower, from whence he never returned, rather than accept of an Honourable imployment, from whence he might not only have returned, but done his friends acceptable service, either in private, or publick.

In his managing of this business (that wisdom which formerly he had been esteemed for) suffered under the censure of Wise men, as well as Fools. Having him now fast in Prison, *Herodias* by pleasing her *Herod* must also ask, and have his life; for, *per seelus ad scelera tutior est via*. To that end they preferred *Emposides* to be servant to Sir *Gervase Elwaies*, then Lieutenant of the Tower, this Gentleman was ever held wise, and honest, but unfortunate in having that place thrust upon him without his thought; he was also so religious, as few in the Court did equal him; so wise, as he obtained that Character of, Wise Sir *Gervase Elwaies*, yet neither could his wisdom, nor the opinion of his religion and honesty, prevent that Fate, he was so ignorant of the Plot, as he never dreamt of any such matter, until one day, as it should seem, *Weston* being told, *Elwaies* did know wherefore he was preferred unto him, to wait on *Overbury*; he asked the Lieutenant, whether he should now do it, *Elwaies* asked him, what? *Weston* at that being somewhat abashed, *Elwaies* espyed it, presently said, no not yet; for he did believe there was something known to *Weston ;* instantly he hasted away (being a little before Dinner) and went into his Study, and sent for *Weston* to come unto him, examining him of the meaning of that question; at last by fair means, and threatning together, got the truth; then *Elwaies*, as he well could, laid before *Weston* the horridness of the Fact, the torments of Hell, and the unassurance of his momentary enjoying, of either reward or favor after the Fact done, but that it must follow, so many Personages of Honor, would never cabinet such a secret in his breast, that might ruine them; at last made him so sensible of his danger in this life, but more sensible of the torments in the other, that *Weston* falling on his knees said; *O Lord, how good and gracious art thou, and thy mercy is above all thy works; for this day is salvation come to my soul, and I would not for all the world have had such a sin upon me:* giving the Lieutenant humble thanks, that had been the instrument of saving his Soul, by putting him off from so foul intentions.

The Lieutenant having now thus renewed grace in him, by making him, as he thought, a new man; thou and I have a dangerous part to act, yet be honest and true to me, and I doubt not, but with Gods help, we shall perform it well, both before God and the world; *Weston* faithfully promised him, and for a long time as faithfully performed with him; the Lieutenant willed him, to bring all such things as were sent him to give *Overbury*, unto him, which he accordingly did; the Lieutenant ever gave them to Cats and Dogs, which he ever had ready in his study for that purpose; some dyed presently, some lay lingering a long time, all which with the Jellies and Tarts sent to *Overbury* he cast into his Privy, they destaining the very Dishes.

This continued long, the Earl ever sending to visit *Overbury*, assuring him he did not forget his release, which should not be long deferred, wherein most men did verily believe he meant both nobly, and truly, though others conjectured his meaning was a dissolution: at last the Countess sent for *Weston*, reviling him, and calling him Treacherous Villain, for had he given those things sent, he had not been now alive; vowing, she would be revenged on him; upon the very fear whereof, he after gave those poysons sent, without acquainting the Lieutenant; yet for all this schooling of *Weston*, and his assurance given of his future fidelity to the Countess, she would not trust him single any more, but put another Co-adjutor to him, one *Frankelin*, a verier Villain then *Weston,* and truly they may be deemed very ill, that could seek out such instruments.

These two Villains came into *Overburies* Chamber, and found him in infinite torment, with contention between the strength of Nature, and the working of the Poyson, and it being very like, Nature had gotten the better in that contention, by the thrusting out of boyls, botches, and blains, they fearing it might come to light, upon the judgement of Phisitians, that foul play had been offered him, consented to stifle him with the Bed-cloaths, which accordingly was performed, and so ended his miserable life, with the assurance of the Conspirators, that he dyed by poyson; none thinking otherwise, but these two Murtherers.

Now was all, as they believed, quiet, and in the depth of security, and the Earl and Countess began to carry their loves more openly, and impudently, so that the world did talk very loudly, and broadly of this adulterous meeting, it must from that ground proceed to an adulterous Marriage, as well to the wronging a young Noble man, as to the dishonor and shame of themselves, *But they must needs goe the Devil drives:* yet know not how, handsomely to effect this, but by making the King a party in this bawdy business, which was no hard matter to effect; for the Kings eye began to wander after a new Favourite, being satiated with the old; therefore for the bringing this bawdry to a Marriage, the Bishops must be principal actors (as I know not in what bad action, they would not be lookers on) and the Bishop of *Winchester,* an excellent Civillian, and a very great Scholler, must be the principal, for which his Son was Knighted; and will never lose that title of Sir *Nullity Bilson.*

For by a nullity of the first Marriage, must this second take place; many meetings of the Bishops and the prime Civillians, in which there wanted no bribes from the Lord, Lady, and their Friends, to have this nullity brought to pass, wherein the Discourse would have better befitted the mouths of Bawds, and Ruffians, then the grave Divines; among them Bishop *Neale,* then Bishop of *Rochester,* a Creature and Favourite of the House of *Suffolk,* took up a learned discourse in the science of Bawdery, how many degrees in that science must produce a Nullity, wherein were so many beastly expressions, as for modesty sake I will not recite them, being offensive to my very thoughts and memory; *Aristotles* Problemes was a modest Discourse to his, and he appeared to be better studied in that, then in Divinity, and to winde up his learned Discourse, concluded, all those met in this Lord, and Lady.

The Arch-Bishop of *Canterbury Abbot*, to his everlasting fame, mainly opposed all the proceedings, and protested against them, for which he ever after lived in disgrace, excluded from the Councel Table, and dyed in the disgrace of the King on Earth, though in favour with the King of Kings.

Yet forsooth to make up the full measure of Bawdery, and to justifie *Neales* Discourse, that all things in the former Marriage conduced to a Nullity, a search must be made, to find whether there had been a penitration, and a Jury of grave Matrons were found fit for that purpose, who with their Spectacles, ground to lesson, not to make the letter larger; after their inspection gave verdict, she was *(intacto vergo)* which was thought very strange, for the world took notice that her way, was very near beaten so plain, as if *(regia via)* and in truth, was a common way before *Somerset* did ever travel that way; besides, the world took notice they two long had lived in Adultery, yet had old *Kettle* a trick for that also.

The Lady of *Essex*, for modesty sake, makes humble suit to the reverend bawdy Bishops, (who were also plotters in this stratagem) that she might not appear bare-faced, for blushing; but desired to come vailed, with a Taffity over her face; this by all means was thought so reasonable, for a pretty modest Lady, that the bawdy Bishops, and pur-blind Ladies, which had forgotten modesty themselves, could not think it worthy the denial; one Mistris *Fines*, near Kinswoman to old *Kettle*, was dressed up in the Countesses Cloathes, at that time too young to be other then *(virgo intacta)* though within two years after, had the old Ladies made their inspection, the orifice would not have appeared so small, to have delivered such a verdict as they did, and a just one upon their view; tho upon some of their knowledges it was not that Lady they were to give verdict upon; if any make doubt of the truth of this Story, the Author delivers upon the reputation of a Gentleman, he had it *verbatim* from a Knight, (otherwise of much Honor, though the very dependency on that Family may question it) which did usher the Lady into the place of inspection, and hath told it often to his friends in mirth.

Now is the Nullity pronounced, and the Marriage with *Somerset* with speed solemnized, for which, they, and the whole Family of *Suffolk* paid dear in after time, and had sower sauce to that sweat meat of their great Son in Law.

And surely he was the most unfortunate man in that Marriage, being as generally beloved for himself, and disposition, as hated afterwards for his linking himself in that family, for in all the Time of this mans favour, before this Marriage he did nothing obnoxious to the State, or any base thing for his private gain, but whether this was his own nature that curbed him, or that there was then a brave Prince living, and a noble Queen that did awe him, we cannot so easily judge, because after this Marriage, and their death, he did many ill things.

In this Favourites flourishing time, came over the *Palsgrave* to marry our Kings Daughter; which for the present, gave much content, and with the general applause, yet it proved a most unfortunate Match to him and his Posterity, and all Christendom, for all his Alliance with so many great Princes, which put on him aspiring thoughts, and was so ambitious as not to content himself, with his hereditary patrimony of one of the greatest Princes in *Germany*; but must aspire to a Kingdom, believing that his great alliance would carry him through any enterprise, or bring him off with honor, in both which he failed; being cast out of his own Country with shame, and he and his, ever after, living upon the devotion of other Princes; but had his Father in Law spent half the mony in Swords he did in words, for which he was but scorned, it had kept him in his own inheritance, and saved much Christian blood since shed; but while he, being wholly addicted to peace, spent much treasure, in sending stately Embassadors to treat his Enemies, (which he esteemed friends) sent armies with a less charge to conquer, so that it may be concluded, that this then thought the most happy Match in Christendom, was the greatest unhappiness to Christendom, themselves and posterity.

And as if to foretel the sad event, presently after the Gallantry, and triumphing of that Marriage, the Kingdom was clad all in mourning, for the sad obsequies of that most hopeful Prince *Henry*, who dyed not without vehement suspicion of Poyson, and I wish I could say suspicion only; but our future discourse will tell you otherwise: He was only shewed to this Nation, as the Land of *Canaan* was to *Moses*, to look on, not to enjoy; we did indeed joy in that happiness we expected in him, but God found us so unthankful, and took so lightly the death of that ever famous Queen *Elizabeth*, as he did intend to make us an example of scorn now, that were formerly of all glory.

His death were foretold by one *Bruce* a most famous Astrologer of the *Scottish* Nation, for which the Earl of *Salisbury*, a great Statesman, caused him to be banished, who left this farewel with the Earl, that it should be too too true, yet his Lordship should not live to see it, the Earl dying in *May*, the Prince in *November* following, to the infinite grief of all the Kingdom; but the Earl of *Somerset* and Family of *Howards*, who by his death thought themselves secured from all future dangers, being a Prince of an open heart, hating all baseness, would often say, if ever he were King, he would not leave one of that Family to piss against a wall.

This brave Prince being dead, *Somerset* and that Faction bear all down before them, disposing of all Offices (yet *Somerset* never turned any out, as the succeding favourite) but places being void, he disposed of them, and who would give most was the word, yet not by *Somerset* himself, but by his Lady and her Family, for he was naturally of a noble disposition, and it may be justly said of him, that could never be said of any before, or ever will be of any after him: He never got suit for himself or friends that was burthensome to the *Common-wealth*, no Monopolies, no Impositions; yet in his time, and by his favor, though not for his use, were brought into the Court two mean fellows, grand Projectors, the one *Ingram*, an ordinary Waiter of the Customs, the other *Cranfield* an Apprentice, who had served three broken Citizens, and its probable by his wit and honesty he might thrive by them all, and lay that for a foundation of his future projecting, the one a brother of *Northamptons*, the other of the house of *Suffolk*, and thus like ill birds defiled their own nests, and discovered the secrets of the Customhouse, yet their projects seemed for the Kings profit only, though much water run by his mill, and *Suffolk* did very well lick his own fingers, for *Salisbury* being dead, *Suffolk* was Treasurer, the proper place for Customs, and his son-in-Law Chamberlain, and Favorite, and then what could not they two do.

Yet *Somerset* ever kept them but like Projectors, which after Favorites, raised to the degrees of Nobility, only *Suffolk* by *Somersets* power made *Ingram* Cofferer of the Kings house, which was the first apparent step to *Somersets* downfal, for however the King made fair semblance to maintain that act, yet made the Earl of *Kelly* his instrument to set the Officers of his household to petition against it, and ever from the Kings own directions to take their instructions, in which one of the principal given, was, not to seek to *Somerset* upon any terms, nay to deny to accept his favor though offered to disanul his own act, but to carry it with an high hand against *Somerset*, by which assurance was given of prevailing, here was pretty jugling; (the Court being then but an

Academy of Juglers,) *Somerset* did often Court the Officers to make him that *Achilles*, his weapon that could wound and heal again, but was entertained with scorn, yet ambition so dazled his eyes, he could not see the *Precipice* on which they stood ready for their downfal, for surely no Astrologers could have given them truer notions of their ruin than this: *Cranfield* the other Projector soared higher, though not in *Somersets* time could he have his feathers imped, but *Buckingham* after did so impe them, that *Cranfield* endeavoured to pull out his and gave him the first affront, by this you may observe how the times altered from better to worse, and so fitest for worthless men.

For now began to appear the glimmering of a new Favorite, one Mr. *George Villers* a younger son by second Venter, of an ancient Knight in *Leicestershire*, as I take it, his Father of an ancient Family, his Mother of a mean, and a waiting Gentlewoman, whom the old man fell in love with and married, by whom he had three sons, all raised to the Nobility, by means of their brother Favourite; this Gentleman was come also but newly from travel, and did believe it a great fortune to marry a Daughter of Sir *Roger Astons*, and in truth was the height of his ambition, and for that only end was an hanger on upon the Court; the Gentlewoman loved him so well, as could all his friends, have made her for her great fortune, but an hundred Marks by Joynter, she had married him presently, in despight of all her friends; and no question would have had him without any Joynture at all.

But before the closing up of this Match, the King cast a glancing eye towards him, which was easily observed by such as observed their Princes humour, and then the match was laid aside, some assuring him a greater Fortune was coming to him, then one gave him his place of Cup-bearer, that he might be in the Kings eye; another sent to his Mercer and Taylor to put good cloathes on him; a third to his Sempster for Curious linnen, and all as in-comes to obtain Offices upon his future rise; then others took upon themselves to be his Braccoes, to undertake his quarrels upon affronts put upon him by *Somersets* Faction, so all hands helped to the piercing up this new Favorite.

Then began the King to eat abroad, who formerly used to eat in his Bed-chamber, or if by chance supped in his Bed-chamber, would come forth to see pastimes and fooleries; in which Sir *Edward Souch*, Sir *George Goring*, and Sir *John Finit*, were the chief and Master Fools, and surely this fooling got them more than any others wisdom, far above them in desert: *Souch* his part to sing bawdy songs; and tell bawdy tales; *Finit* to compose these Songs; then were a set of Fidlers brought up on purpose for this Fooling, and *Goring* was master of the game for Fooleries; sometimes presenting *David Droman,* and *Archer Armstrong* the Kings Fools, on the back of the other fools, to tilt one at another, till they fell together by the ears; sometimes Antick Dances, but Sir *John Millisert,* who was never known before, was commended for notable Fooling, and so was the best extemporary Fool of them all; with this jollity was this Favorite ushered in, this made the House of *Suffolk* fret, and *Somerset* carried himself more proudly, and his Bravado's, ever quarrelling with the others, which by his Office of Lord *Chamberlain* for a while carried it, but *Somersets* using of Sir *Ralph Wynhood,* (whom himself brought in for Secretary of State) in so scornful a manner (he having only the title, the Earl himself keeping the Seals, and doing the business) made *Wynhood* endeavour to ruine him, who soon got an opportunity by frequenting the Countess of *Shrewsbury,* then prisoner in the Tower, who told *Wynhood* on a time, that *Overbury* was poysoned, which she understood from Sir *Gervase Elwaies ;* who did labor by her means to deal with her two sons in-law, *Arundel* and *Pembroke,* (*Wynhood* also being great with that faction) that when it came into question, he might save his own stake, who truly was no otherwise guilty, but that he did not discover it at *Westerns* first disclosing it, the being keeper of the Prison, so by inference not disclosing it, was *Overburies* death; and had he revealed it then, I dare say he had been brought into the *Star-chamber* for it, and undone (for yet was not the time fit for discovery,) *Wynhood,* it was thought, acquainted the King with it, knowing how willingly he would have been rid of *Somerset,* yet the King durst not bring it in question, nor any question ever would have been, had not *Somerset* sought to cross him in his passion of love to his new Favorite, in which the King was more impatient then any woman to enjoy her love.

Not long after *Thrumbel* Agent at *Bruxels,* had by an Apothecaries boy one *Reeve,* after an Apothecary himself in *London,* and dyed very lately, gotton hold of this poysoning business, for *Reeve* having under his Master, made some of those desperate Medicines, either run away, or else his Master sent him out of the way, and fell in company of *Thrumbels* servant at *Bruxels,* to whom he revealed it, they to their Master, who examining the boy discovered the truth; *Thrumbel* presently wrote to Secretary *Wynhood* he had business of consequence to dicover, but would not send it, therefore desired licence to come over. The King would not yield to his return, but willed him to send an express; that *Thrumbal* utterly refused, and very wisely, for letting any thing appear under his hand, least the boy should dye, or run away, and then himself made the Author of that, which the courtesie of another must have justified.

The King being of a longing disposition, rather then he would not know, admitted *Thrumbals* return, and now had they good testimony by the Apothecary, who revealed *Weston*, Mrs. *Turner*, and *Franklyn*, to be principal Agents, yet this (being now the time of progress) was not stirred till about *Michaelmas*; yet *Wyndhood* did now carry himself in a braving way of contestation against *Somerset*, struck in with the Faction of *Villers*, and now on progress. The King went Westward where he was feasted at *Cranborn*, by a son in law of that Family; at *Ludworth* and *Binden*, by the Lord *Walden*; at *Charlton* by Sir *Thomas Howard*; and nothing but one Faction braving the other; then was the King feasted at *Purbeck* by the Lord *Hatton*, who was of the contrary Faction, and at a Joynture house of Sir *George Villers* Mother, called *Gotly*, where he was magnificently entertained.

After all this feasting, homeward came the King, who desired by all means to reconcile this clashing between his declining and rising Favorite; to which end, at *Lulworth* the King imployed Sir *Humfrey May*, a great servant to *Somerset*, and a wise servant to *Villers*; but with such instructions, as if came from himself, and *Villers* had order presently after Sir *Humfrey May's* return, to present himself and service to *Somerset*. "My Lord, Sir *George Villers* will come to you to offer his service, and desire to be your creature; and therefore refuse him not, embrace him, and your Lordship shall still stand a great man, though not the sole Favorite: My Lord seemed averse, Sir *Humfrey* then told him in plain terms, that he was sent by the King to advise it, and that *Villers* would come to him to cast himself into his protection, to take his rise under the shadow of his wings: Sir *Humfrey May* was not parted from my Lord half an hour, but in comes Sir *George Villers*, and used these very words, " My Lord, I desire to be your servant, and your creature, and shall desire to take my Court-preferment under your favor and your Lordship shall find me as faithful a servant unto you as ever did serve you." My Lord returned this quick and short answer, " I will none of your service, and you shall none of my favor, I will, if I can, break your neck, and of that be confident." This was but an harsh Complement, and savored more of spirit than wisdom; and since that time breaking each others necks was their aims, and it's verily believed, had *Somerset* complied with *Villers*, *Overbury's* death had still layn raked up in his own ashes; but God, who will never suffer murther to go unpunished, will have what he will, maugre all the wisdom of the World.

To *Windsor* doth the King return, to end his progress, from thence to *Hampton-Court*, then to *White-hall*, and shortly after to *Royston*, to begin his Winter-Journey.

And now begins the Game to be plaid, in which *Somerset* must be the loser, the Cards being shuffled, cut, and dealt, between the King and Sir *Edward Cook*, chief Justice, whose daughter *Purbeck, Villers* had married, or was to marry, and therefore a fit instrument to ruin *Somerset*, and Secretary *Wynhood*; these all plaid the stake, *Somersets* life, and his Ladies, and their fortunes, and the Family of *Suffolk*; some of them played booty, and in truth, the Game was not plaid above board. The day the King went from *White-hall*, to *Theobalds*, and so to *Royston*, the King sent for all the Judges (his Lords and Servants encircling him,) where kneeling down in the midst, he used these words:

"My Lords, the Judges; it is lately come to my hearing, that you have now in examination a business of poysoning, Lord in what a most miserable condition shall this Kingdom be, (the only famous nation for hospitality in the world) if our tables should become such a snare, as none could eat without danger of his life, and that *Italian* custom should be introduced amongst us; therefore, my Lords, I charge you, as you will answer it at that great and dreadful day of Judgment, that you examine it strictly without favor, affection, or partiality; and if you shall spare any guilty of this crime, Gods curse light on you and your posterity: And if I spare any that are found guilty, Gods curse light on me and my posterity for ever." But how this dreadful thunder-curse or imprecation was performed, shall be shewed hereafter; and I pray God, the effect be not felt amongst us even at this day (as it hath been, I fear on that vertuous Lady *Elizabeth*, and her children,) for God treasures up such imprecations and deprecations, and pours them out, when a Nation least dreams, even when they cry, Peace, peace, to their souls; and it may well be (at this time our other sins concurring) pouring out upon King, Judges, and the whole State.

It appears how unwilling the King was to ruine *Somerset*, a creature of his own making, *sed immedicable vulnus, Ense rescindendum est*. Grace was offered by the King, had he had grace to have apprehended it.

The King with this, took his farewel for a time of *London*, and was accompanied with *Somerset* to *Royston* (where no sooner he brought him) but instantly took leave, little imagining what viper lay amongst the herbs; nor must I forget to let you know how perfect the King was in the art of dissimulation, or to give it his own phrase *(King-craft;)* The Earl of *Somerset* never parted from him with more seeming affection than at this time, when he knew *Somerset* should never see him more; and had you seen that seeming affection (as the Author himself did) you would rather have believed he was in his rising, than setting. The Earl when he kissed his hand, the King hung about his neck, slabboring his cheeks; saying, for Gods sake, when shall I see thee again; On my soul, I shall neither eat nor sleep until you come again; the Earl told him, on Monday (this being on the Friday,) for Gods sake let me said the King, shall I, shall I? Then lolled about his neck; then, for Gods sake, give thy lady this kiss for me; in the same manner at the stayres head, at the middle of the stayres, and at the stayres foot; the Earl was not in his coach, when the King used these very words (in the hearing of four Servants, of whom one was *Somersets* great creature, and of the Bed-chamber, who reported it instantly to the Author of this History) I shall never see his face more. I appeal to the Reader, whether his Motto of, *Qui nescit dissimulare nescit regnare*, was not as well performed in this passage as his *Beati pacifici*, in the whole course of his life; and his love to the latter, made him to be beaten with his own weapon in the other, by all Princes and States that had to do with him.

But before *Somersets* approach to *London*, his Countess was apprehended, at his arrival, himself; and the King being that time at supper, said to Sir *Thomas Monson*, My Lord Chief Justice has sent for you; he asked the King when he should wait upon him again; who replied, you may come when you can: And (as in the story of *Byron*, and many others) there have been many foolish observations, as presage, so was there in this Gentleman, who was the Kings Mr. Faulconer, and in truth such a one, as no Prince in Christendom had; for what Flights other Princes had, he would excel them for his Master, in which one was at the Kite.

The *French* sending over his Faulconers to shew that sport, his Master Faulconer lay long here, but could not kill one Kite, ours being more magnanimous then the French Kite; Sir *Thomas Monson* desired to have that flight in all exquisiteness, and to that end was at 1000*l*. charge in Gos-Faulcons for that flight, in all that charge, he never had but one cast would perform it, and those had killed nine Kites never missed one. The Earl of *Pembroke* with all the Lords, desired the King but to walk out of *Roysten* Towns end, to see that flight, which was one of the most stately flights of the world, for the high mountee; the King went unwillingly forth, the flight was shewed, but the Kite went to such a mountee, as all the field lost sight of Kite, and Hawk and all, and neither Kite nor Hawk were either seen or heard of to this present, which made all the Court conjecture it a very ill *omen*.

So that you see, the plot was so well laid, as they should be all within the toyle at one instant, not knowing of each other. Now are in hold, the Earl, his Countess, Sir *Thomas Monson*, Mistris *Turner* (a very lewd and infamous woman of life) *Weston* and *Franklyn*, with some others of less note, of which one *Symon*, a servant of Sir *Thomas Monson*, who was imployed in carrying Jelly and Tart to the Tower, who upon his examination, for his pleasant answer, was instantly dismissed. My Lord told him, *Symon* you have had a hand in this poysoning business; No, my good Lord, I had but one finger in it, which almost cost me my life, and at the best cost me all my hair and nails; for the truth was, *Symon* was somewhat liquorish, and finding the sirrup swim from the top of a Tart as he carried, he did with his finger skim it off, and it was to be believed, had he known what it had been, he would not have been his taster at so dear a rate; and that you may know *Symons* interest with that Family, I shall tell you a true story.

Sir *Thomas Monson* was a great lover of Musick, and had as good as *England* had, especially for voyces, and was at infinite charge in breeding some in *Italy*. This *Symon* was an excellent Musician, and did sing delicately, but was a more general Musician than ever the world had; He had a *Catro* of immense length and bigness, with this, being his Tabor stick, the palm of his hand his Tabor, and his mouth his pipe, he would so imitate a Tabor Pipe, as if it had been so indeed: To this Music would Mrs. *Turner*, the young Ladies, and some of that Gig, dance ever after supper; the old Lady, who loved that Musick as well as her daughters, would sit and laugh, she could scarce sit for laughing; and it was believed, that some of them danced after that pipe without the Tabor, his master coming to hear of it, turned him away, but was infinitely importuned to take him again, he could not have wanted a service, but he never durst use his pipe amongst them, for their dancing recreation, however he might for any other.

F

And now poor Mrs. *Turner*,* *Weston*, and *Franklyn* began the Tragedy, Mrs. *Turners* day of mourning being better than the day of her birth, for she died very penitently, and shewed much modesty in her last act, which is to be hoped was accepted by *God*; after that dyed *Weston*; and then was *Franklyn* arraigned, who confessed that *Overbury* was smothered to death, not poysoned to death, though he had poyson given him.

Here was *Cook*, glad, how to cast about to bring both ends together, Mrs. *Turner* and *Weston* being already hanged for killing *Overbury* with poyson, but he being the very quintessence of Law, presently informs the Jury, that if a man be done to death with Pistols, Poniards, Swords, Halter, Poyson, &c. so he be done to death, the Indictment is good, if but indicted for any of those ways, but the good Lawyers of those times were not of that opinion, but did believe that Mrs. *Turner* was directly murthered by my Lord *Cooks* Law, as *Overbury* was without any Law.

In the next place, comes the Countess to her tryal; at whose Arraignment, as also at Mrs. *Turners* before, were shewn many Pictures, Puppits, with some exorcism and Magick spells, which made them appear more odious, as being known to converse with Witches and Wizzards; and amongst the tricks, *Formans* book was shewed, this *Forman* was a fellow dwelt in *Lambeth*, a very silly fellow,† yet had wit enough to cheat Ladies, and other women, by pretending skill in telling their Fortunes, as whether they should bury their husbands, and what second husband they should have, and whether they should enjoy their Loves, or whether Maids should get husbands, or enjoy their servants to themselves without Corrivals; but before he would tell any thing, they must write their names to his Alphabetical book, with their own hand-writing; by this trick he kept them in awe, if they should

---

* When Lord Chief Justice Coke pronounced sentence of death on Mrs. Turner, he said, "That as she was the first inventress and wearer of yellow starched ruffs and cuffs, so he hoped, she would be the last that wore them, and for that purpose strictly charged, she should be hanged in that garb, that the fashion might end in shame and detestation." His hope was fully accomplished, as never after from the day she was executed, was the yellow ruff or cuff, seen to be worn.

† He was a chandler's son in the city of Westminster. He travelled into Holland for a month in 1580, purposely to be instructed in astrology, and other more occult sciences; as also in physic, taking his degree of Doctor beyond seas: being sufficiently furnished and instructed with what he desired, he returned into England, towards the latter end of the reign of Queen Elizabeth, and flourished until that year of King James,

complain of his abusing them, as in truth he did nothing else: Besides, it was believed, some meetings was at his house, and that the Art of Bawd was more beneficial to him, then that of a Conjurer; and that he was a better Artist in the one, then the other; and that you may know his skill, he was himself a Cuckold, having a very pretty wench to his wife, which would say she did it to try his skill, but it fared with him as it did with Astrologers, that cannot foresee their destiny. I well remember there was much mirth made in the Court, upon shewing this book, for it was reported, the first leaf my Lord *Cook* lighted on, he found his own wives name.

 The next that came on the stage was Sir *Thomas Monson*; but the night before he was to come to his tryal, the King being at the game of Maw, said, To morrow comes *Thomas Monson* to his tryal; yea, said the Kings Card-holder, where if he do not play his Masters prize, your Majesty shall never trust me; this so run in the Kings mind, at the next game, he said he was sleepy, and would play out that set next night; the Gentleman departed to his lodging, but was no sooner gone, but the King sent for him, what communication they had, I know not, (yet it may be, can more easily guess then any other,) but it is most certain, next under God, that Gentleman saved his life, for the King sent a Post presently to *London*, to let the Lord chief Justice know, he would see

---

wherein the Countess of Essex, the Earl of Somerset and Sir Thomas Overbury's matters were questioned. He lived in Lambeth with a very good report of the neighbourhood, especially of the poor, unto whom he was charitable. He was a person that in horary questions, (especially thefts) was very judicious and fortunate; so also in sickness, which indeed was his master piece. In resolving questions about marriage he had good success; in other questions very moderate. He was a person of indefatigable pains. I have seen sometimes half one sheet of paper wrote of his judgment upon one question; in writing whereof he used much tautology, as you may see yourself, (most excellent Esquire) if you read a great book of Dr. Flood's which you have, who had all that book from the manuscripts of Foreman; for I have seen the same word for word in an English manuscript formerly belonging to Doctor Willoughby of Gloucestershire.

Now we come to his death, which happened as follows: the Sunday night before he died, his wife and he being at supper in their garden-house, she being pleasant, told him that she had been informed he could resolve, whether man or wife should die first; Whether shall I (quoth she) bury you or no? Oh Trunco, for so he called her, thou wilt bury me, but thou will much repent it. Yea, but how long first? I shall die, said he, ere Thursday Night. Monday came, all was well. Tuesday came, he not sick. Wednesday came, and still he was well; with which his impertinent wife did much twit him in the teeth. Thursday came, and dinner was ended, he very well; he went down to the water side, and took a pair of oars to go to some buildings he was in hand with in Puddle Dock. Being in the middle of the Thames, he presently fell down, only saying, An impost, an impost, and so died. A most sad storm of wind immediately following.

Monsons examination and confession, to see if it were worthy to touch his life, for so small a matter; *Monson* was too wise to set any thing but fair confession, what he would have stab'd with, should have been (*viva voce*) at his Arraignment. The King sent word, he see nothing worthy of death, or of bonds, in his Accusation or Examination: *Cook* was so mad, he could not have his will of *Monson*, that he said, Take him away we have other matters against him of an higher nature; with which words, out issues about a dozen Warders of the Tower, and took him from the Bar; and *Cooks* malice was such against him, as though it rained extreamly and *Monson* not well, he made him goe a foot from the *Guild-hall* to the Tower, which almost cost him his life; there lay he a close prisoner above three months, the end to get a Recorders place (that *Cranfield* desired) every man thinking him in some treason, would not lend him mony, and if so much mony had not been paid by such a time, his place had been forfeited. And in this let me commend the part of a true friend in Sir *Hum. May*, who at 24 hours, made his brother *Herick* take up 2000l. and pay it, to save his office, without so much as any security from Sir *Thomas Monson* (for he was close prisoner,) or from any friend of his; and that you may know it was for his Office, this hard measure was shewed him, the Money was no sooner paid, but his friends might come unto him; and I must not let pass the skill of the Lord *Loreskeine*, a Scotchman, who long before, by his physiognomy, told Sir *G. Marshall*, that Sir *Thomas Monson* would escape hanging neerer then ever any man did; which was true, for he was twice brought to his trial, put himself both times upon his Country, yet was only indicted, never tried, and yet had he harder measure then ever any man had, for he lost his Office, being but indicted, and not condemned, which is without any president.

And now for the last act, enters *Sommerset* himself on the Stage who (being told, as the manner is, by the Lieutenant, that he must provide to go next day to his tryal) did absolutely refuse it, and said, they should carry him in his bed; that the King had assured him, he should not come to any tryal, neither durst the King to bring him to tryal; this was in an high strain, and in a language not well understood by *George Moore* (Lieutenant in *Elwaies* his room) that made *Moore* quiver and shake, and however he was accounted a wise man, yet was he neer at his wits end.

Yet away goes *Moore* to *Greenwich*, as late as it was (being 12 in night) bounseth at the back stayres as if mad, to whom came *Jo. Loveston*, one of the Grooms out of his bed, enquires the reason of that distemper at so late a season; *Moore* tells him he must speak with the King; *Loveston* replyes, he is quiet (which in the Scottish dialect, is fast asleep) *Moore* says you must awake him; *Moore* was called in, (the Chamber left to the King and *Moore*) he tells the King those passages, and desired to be directed by the King, for he was gone beyond his own reason, to hear such bold and undutiful expressions, from a faulty Subject, against a just Soveraign; The King falls into a passion of tears, On my soul, *Moore*, I wot not what to do, thou art a wise man, help me in this great straight, and thou shalt find thou dost it for a thankfull Master, with other sad expressions; *Moore* leaves the King in that passion, but assures him he will prove the utmost of his wit, to serve his Majesty, and was really rewarded with a suit worth to him 1500*l*. although *Annundale* his great friend, did cheat him of one half, so was there falshood in friendship.

Sir *George Moore* returns to *Somerset* about three next morning, of that day he was to come to trial, enters *Somersets* chamber, tells him he had been with the King, found him a most affectionate Master unto him, and full of grace in his intentions towards him, but (said he) to satisfie Justice, you must appear, although return instantly again, without any further proceeding, only you shall know your enemies and their malice, though they shall have no power over you: With this trick of wit, he allayed his fury, and got him quietly, about eight in the morning to the Hall, yet feared his former bold language might revert again, and being brought by this trick into the toile, might have inraged him to fly out into some strange discovery, that he had two servants placed on each side of him, with a Cloake on their arms, giving them a peremptory order, if that *Somerset* did any way fly out on the King, they should instantly hoodwink him with that Cloak, take him violently from the Bar, and carry him away; for which, he would secure them from any danger, and they should not want also a bountiful reward. But the Earl finding himself over-reached, recollected a better temper, and went on calmly in his Tryal, where he held the company till 7 at night. But who had seen the Kings restless motion all that day, sending to every Boat he see landing at the Bridge, cursing all that came without tydings, would have easily judged all was not right, and there had been some grounds for *Somersets* boldness; but at last bringing him word he was condemned, and the passages, All was quiet. This is the very relation from *Moores* own mouth, and this told to two Gentlemen (of which the Author was one) that had had no assurance of their honesty, but though he failed in his wisdom, or rather doted at this instant, yet they failed not in that worth inherent in every Noble spirit, never speaking of it till the Kings death, both the Gentlemen being now alive, and had this *verbatim* from *Moore* in *Wanstead* Park.

And there were other strong inducements, to believe *Somerset* knew that by him, he desired none other in the world should be partaker of, and that all was not peace within the Peace-Maker himself; for he ever courted *Somerset* to his dying day, and gave him 4000*l. per annum* for *Fearne resits*, after he was condemned, which he took in his servants names, not his own (as then being condemned, not capable of) and he then resolved never to have pardoned. I have heard it credibly reported, he was told by a Wizzard, that could he but come to see the Kings face again, he should be reinvested in his former dearness; this had been no hard experiment, but belike he had too much Religion, to trust to Wizzards, or else some friends of his had trusted them, and been deceived by them, that he had little reason to put confidence in them.

Many believe him guilty of *Overburies* death, but the most thought him guilty only of the breach of Friendship (and that in a high point) by suffering his imprisonment, which was the high way to his murther; and this conjecture I take to be of the soundest opinion; for by keeping him out of the action (if it were discovered) his greatness fortified with innocency, would carry their nocensies through all dangers; for the Gentleman himself, he had misfortune, to marry such a Woman, in such a family, which first undermined his honour, afterwards his life (at least to be dead in law;) nor did any thing reflect upon him in all his time of Favorite, but in, and by that family; first in his adulterous marriage, then in so hated a Family, and the bringing in *Cranfield* and *Ingram*, as Projectors, all by his wives and friends means; otherwise, had he been the bravest Favorite of our time, full of Majesty, imploying his time like a Statesman, and the King kept correspondency with him by Letters, almost weekly, to his dying day.

And here we have brought this great man to his end, with his Countess, Mrs. *Turner, Weston, Franklyn,* and *Elwaies* dyed in the Tower, and here dyed this great business, *Weston* ever saying, it never troubled him, to dye with so many blue ribbonds; and its verily believed, when the King made those terrible imprecations on himself, Deprecations of the judges, it was intended the Law should run in its proper channel, but was stopt and put out of course by the folly of that great Clerk, Sir *Edward Cook*, though no wise man, who in a vain glorious speech, to shew his vigilency, enters into a rapture as he sat on the Bench, saying God knows what become of that sweet babe Prince Henry, (but I know somewhat;) and surely in searching the Cabinets, he lighted on some Papers, that spake plain in that which was ever whispered, which, had he gone on in a gentle way, would have falen in of themselves, not to have been prevented, but this folly of his tongue, stopt the breath of that discovery, of that so foul a murder, which I fear, cryes still for vengeance.

And now begins the new Favorite to reign, without any controlement; now he rises in honour, as well as swells with pride, being broken out of the modest bounds, formerly had impayled him, to the high-way of pride and scorn, turning out, and putting in all he pleased; First he must aspire to the Admirals Office himself, and would not let the old Gentleman (so well deserving in that place) dye with that Title, but the King must put himself to a great charge, to put out the better, and take in the worse; yet for all his immense greatness, would never let him be Admiral until he had first settled Sir *Robert Mansel* Vice-Admiral of *England*, during his life by Patent, in which, he not only manifested his love to his Noble Friend, though sometime his servant, but his care to the State, that his experience and abilities might support the others inabilities; well-knowing that the Honor and Safety of the Kingdom, consisted in the well ordering and strength of the *Navy*.

Next *Egerton* had displeased him, not giving way to his exorbitant desires, he must out, and would not let him seal up his dying eyes, which he had so long carried, and so well discharged; and to despite him the more, and to vex his very soul in the last agony, he sent *Bacon*, his desired Successor (one he hated) for the Seals, which the old mans spirit could not brook, but sent them by his own servant to the King, and shortly afterwards yielded his soul to his Maker.

And to the end you may know what men were made choyce of, to serve turns, I shall set you down a true Story: This great Favorite sent a Noble Gentleman, and of much worth, to *Bacon* with this Message, that he knew him to be a man of excellent parts, and as the times were, fit to serve his Master in the Keepers place, but he also knew him of a base and ingrateful disposition, and an arrant knave, apt in his prosperity, to ruin any that had raised him from adversity; yet for all this, he did so much study his Masters service (knowing how fit an instrument he might be for him) that he had obtained the Seals for him; but with this assurance, should he ever requite him, as he had done some others, to whom he had been more bound, he would cast him down as much below scorn, as he had now raised him high above any Honor he could ever have expected.

Bacon, being then Atturney, patiently hearing this Message, replyed, I am glad my Noble Lord deals so friendly and freely with me, and hath made that choyse of so discreet and Noble a friend, to convey it unto me, and that had delivered the Message in so plain language; but, saith he, can my Lord know these abilities in me, and can he think when I have attained the highest preferment my profession is capable of, I shall so much fail in my judgment, and understanding, as to lose these abilities? and by my miscarriage to so noble a Patron, cast myself headlong from the top of that honor to the very bottom of contempt and scorn? Surely, my Lord cannot think so meanly of me. The Gentleman replyed, I deliver you nothing from my self, but the words are put into my mouth by his Lordship, to which I neither add nor diminish; for had it been left to my discretion, surely, though I might have given you the substance, yet should I have apparelled it in a more modest attire; but as I have faithfully delivered my Lords to you, so will I as faithfully return yours to his Lordship.

You must understand the reason of this Message, was his ungratefulness to *Essex*, which every one could remember, for the Earl saved him from starving, and he requited him so, as his Apology must witness; were there not a great fault, there needed no Apology; nor could any age, but a worthless, and corrupt in men and manners, have thought him worthy such a place of honor.

Well, Lord Keeper he was for which he paid nothing, nor was he able; for now was there a new trick to put in dishonest and necessitous men, to serve such turnes, as men of plentiful fortunes, and fair reputations, would not accept of; and this filled the Church and Common-wealth full of beggerly fellows (such daring to venture on any thing) having nothing to lose; (for it is riches makes men coward; Poverty, daring and valiant, to adventure at any thing to get something) yet did not *Buckingham* do things *gratis*, but what their purses could not stretch unto, they paid in pensions out of their places, all which went to maintain his numerous beggerly kindred; *Bacon* payed a pension; *Heath* Atturney paid a pension, *Margrave* Dean, paid a Pension, with many others: Nor was this any certain rule, for present portions must be raised; of a poor Kitchin-Maid, to be made a great Countess; for *Fotherby* made Bishop of *Sarum*, paid 3500*l*. and some also, worthy men, were preferred *gratis*, to blow up their Fames, and Trumpet forth their Nobleness (as *Tolson*, a worthy man, paid nothing in Fine or pension; after him, *Davenat*, in the same Bishoprick;) but these were but as Musick before ev'ry bound; nor were fines or pensions certain, but where men were rich, there Fines without reservation of rent; where poor, and such as would serve turns, their pensions, no Fines; so *Weston*, and many others: There were books of rates on all Offices, Bishopricks, Deanries in *England*, that could tell you what Fines, what Pensions, otherwise had it been impossible such a numerous kindred could have been maintained with three Kingdoms Revenue.

Now was *Bacon* invested in his Office, and within ten days after the King goes to *Scotland*; *Bacon* instantly begins to believe himself King, lyes in the Kings Lodgings, gives audience in the great Banqueting house, makes all other Councellors attend his motions, with the same state the King used to come out, to give audience to Embassadors; when any other Councellor sate with him about the Kings affairs, would (if they sate near him) bid them know their distance; upon which, *Wynhood*, Secretary, rose, went away, and would never sit more, but instantly dispatcht one to the King, to desire him to make hast back, for his Seat was already usurped: At which, I remember, the King reading it unto us, both the King and we were very merry; and if *Buckingham* had sent him any Letter, would not vouchsafe the opening or reading in publick, tho it was said, it required speedy dispatch, nor would vouchsafe him any answer. In this posture he lived, until he heard the King was returning, and began to believe the Play was almost at an end, he might personate a Kings part no longer, and therefore did again re-invest with his old rags of baseness, which were so tattered and poor at the Kings coming to *Windsor*; he attended two days at *Buckinghams* Chamber, being not admitted to any better place, then the room where trencher-scrapers and Laquies attended, there sitting upon an old wooden chest, (amongst such as for his baseness, were only fit for his companions, although the Honor of his place did merit far more respect) with his Purse and Seal lying by him on that chest; My self told a servant of my Lord of *Buckinghams*, it was a shame to see the Purse and Seal of so little value, or esteem in his Chamber, though the Carryer without it, merited nothing but scorn, being worst among the basest. He told me they had command it must be so; after two days he had admittance; at first entrance, fell down flat on his face at the Dukes foot, kissing it, vowing never to rise till he had his pardon, then was he again reconciled, and since that time so very a slave to the Duke, and all that Family, that he durst not deny the command of the meanest of the kindred, nor oppose any thing; by this you see, a base spirit is ever most concomitant with the proudest mind, and surely never so many parts, and so base and abject a spirit, tenated together in any one earthen Cottage, as in this one man: I shall not remember his baseness, being out of his place, of pinning himself, for very scraps, on that Noble Gentleman, Sir *Julius Cæsars* Hospitality, that at last he was forced to get the Kings Warrant to remove him out of his house; yet in his prosperity, the one being Chancellor, and the other Master of the Rolls, did so scorn and abuse him, as he would alter any thing the other did.

And now *Buckingham* having the Chancellor, Treasurer, and all great Officers his very slaves, swells in the height of pride, summons up all the Country kindred, the old Countess providing a place for them to learn to carry themselves in a Court-like garb, but because they could not learn the French Dances so soon as to be in gay clothes, Country Dances must be the garb of the Court and none else must be used.

Then must these women kindred be married to Earls, Earls eldest sons, Barons, or chief Gentlemen of greatest estates, insomuch that the very female kindred were so numerous, as sufficient to have peopled any Plantation; nay, very Kitchen-wenches were married to Knights eldest sons; yet, as if *England* had not matches enough in the Kingdom, they married like the house of *Austria*, in their own kindred, witness the Earl of *Anglice*, married a cousen Jerman, to whom he had given earnest before; so that King *James*, that naturally, in former times, hated women, had his Lodgings replenished with them, and all of the kindred. The Brethren, great Earls. Little children did run up and down the Kings Lodgings, like little Rabbit-starters about their boroughs: Here was a strange change, that the King, who formerly would not endure his Queen and Children in his Lodgings, now you would have judged, that none but women frequented them; nay, that was not all, but the kindred had all the houses about *White-Hall* (as if Bulwarks and Flankers about that Cittadale.) But above all, the miracles of those times, old Sir *Anthony Ashley*, who never loved any but boys, yet he was snatcht up for a kinswoman, as if there had been a concurrency through the Kingdom, that those that naturally hated women, yet loved his kindred, as well as the King him.

And the very old Midwives of that kindred, flockt up for preferment, of which, old Sir *Christopher Perkins*, a women hater, that never meant to marry, nay it was said, he had made a vow of Virginity, yet was coupled to an old Midwife; so that you see the greatness of this Favourite, who could force (by his power over the King) though against Nature.

But I must tell you, this got him much hatred, to raise brothers, and brothers-in-law to the highest rank of Nobility, which were not capable of the place, scarce of a Justice of the peace, only *Purbeck* had more wit and honesty than all the kindred beside, and did keep him in some bounds of honesty and modesty, whilst he lived about him, and would speak plain English to him; for which plainness, when they had no colour to put him from his brother, they practised to make him mad, and thought to bring that wicked stratagem to effect, by countenancing a wicked woman, his wife, the Lord *Cooks* daughter against him, even in her base and lewd living.

And now is *Purbeck* mad, and put from Court, now none great with *Buckingham*, but Bawds and Parasites, and such as humored him, in his unchast pleasures; so that since his first being a pretty, harmless, affable Gentleman, he grew insolent, cruel, and a monster not to be endured.

And now is *Williams*, sometimes Chaplain to Lord Keeper *Egerton*, brought into play, made a Privy-Councellor, Dean of *Westminster*, and of secret Councel with the King, he was also made Bishop of *Lincolne*, and was generally voyced at his first step, to marry *Buckinghams* mother, who was in her husbands time, created a Countess, he remaining still a silly drunken sot, and this was the first president of this kind ever known. *Williams* held her long in hand, and no doubt, in nature of her Confessor, was her secret friend, yet would not marry, which afterwards was cause of his downfal at the present.

Then was there a Parliament summoned, in which, *Bacon* for his bribery and injustice, was thrust out, being closely prosecuted by one *Morby* a Woodmonger, and one *Wrenham*, formerly deeply censured, *Bacon* was by Parliament justly put out of his place, and but only for the Votes of the Bishop, had been degraded; the Bishops might have done better to have kept their voyces to have done themselves service at this time, but surely that, with some other injustice of theirs, had so filled up their measure of iniquity, that now Gods anger is kindled against them.

In *Bacons* place come *Williams*, a man on purpose brought in at first to serve turns, but in this place to do that which none of the Laity could be found bad enough to undertake, whereupon this observation was made, that first no Lay-man could be found so dishonest as a Clergy-man; next, as *Bacon* the father of this *Bacon*, did receive the Seals from a Bishop, so a Bishop again received them from a *Bacon*; and at this did the Lawyers fret, to have such a flower pulled out of their Garland.

This *Williams*, though he wanted much of his Predecessors abilities for the Law, yet did he equal him for learning and pride, and beyond him in the way of bribery, this man answering by petitions, a new way, in which his servants had one part, himself another, and so was calculated to be worth to him and his servants 3000l. *per annum*, a new way never found out before.

And now being come to the height of his preferment, he did estrange himself from the company of the old Countess, having much younger ware, who had keys to his chamber, to come to him, yet was their a necessity of keeping him in this place for a time, the *Spanish* Match being yet in chase, and if it succeeded, this man was to clap the Great Seal (through his ignorance in the Laws) to such things that none that understood the danger by knowing the Laws, would venture upon, and for this design was he at first brought in, (no Prince living knowing how to make use of men, better than King *James*.)

Now was also *Suffolk* turned out of his place of Lord Treasurer, and a fellow of the same hatch that *Williams* was brought into his place, *Cranfield* that was the Projector, and never could get higher than that title in *Somersets* time, now marrying one of *Buckinghams* kindred, so that it was now generally said, that for pride and baseness these two great places were never so fitted, both of mean birth, both proud, only the one an excellent Scholler, and of great parts; the other, nothing but a pack of ignorance sawthered together with imprudence to raise him (besides his marriage in the lusty kindred.)

This *Cranfield* was a fellow of so mean a condition, as none but a poor spirited Nobility would have endured his perching on that high Tree of Honor, to the dishonour of the Nobility, the disgrace of the Gentry, and not long after to his own dishonor, who was thrust out of the Lords House with this censure, that thou Lionel, Earl of Middlesex, shalt never sit, or have voyce more in this House of Peers, and shalt pay for a fine to our Soveraign Lord the King 20000l. leaving him still to overtop the Gentry, the Bishops kept him also from degrading, which I do verily believe is one cause the Gentry will degrade them.

The *Spanish* Match, having been long in Treaty, and it being suspected now, that the *Spaniard* did juggle with this State in this, as

OF KING JAMES.

they formerly did in a Match with that brave Prince *Henry*, and in truth, in all other things wherein any negotiation had been, only feeding the King with fair hopes, and fair words, yet foul deeds. Whether the King suspected any such matter, or any whimsey came in the brain of this great Favorite and Prince, to imitate the old stories of the Knights Errand, but agreed it was (it should seem) between the Favorite and the Prince only (no one other so much as dreaming of any such adventure) except *Cottington*, who also accompanied them, that the Prince must go himself into *Spain;* away they went under the borrowed names of *Jack* and *Tom Smith* to the amazement of all wise men, only accompanied with *Cottington*, and some one or two more at most, taking their way by *France;* had the Ports laid so, that none should follow them, or give any notice to the *French* Court, till they might get the start, &c. yet their wisdoms made them adventure to stay in the *French* Court, and look on that Lady whom he after married; and there did this *Mars* imitate one of Prince *Arthurs* Knights, in seeking Adventures through forreign Princes territories; 1st beheld this *French* beauty *Mars vidit visamq; cupit potiturq; cupita:* as in our discourse will afterward appear; from thence away to *Spain;* but as the Journy was only plotted by young heads, so it was so childishly carried, that they escaped the *French* Kings Curriers very narrowly, but escape they did, and arrived safely in *Spain* their wished Port, before either welcome, or expected, by our Embassadors, or that State.

Yet now must the best face be put on, at all hands, that put their Grandees to new shifts, and our Embassador the Earl of *Bristol* to try his wit, for at that time was Sir *Walter Aston* also Embassador at *Spain*, in all occurrences *Aston* complyed with the Prince and Duke, *Bristol* ran counter; and the Duke and *Bristol* hated each other mortally.

Bristol had the advantage of them there, as having the much better head-peece, and being more conversant and dear with that state, wholly complying with them, and surely had done them very acceptable services (and in this very Treaty was one of the pack) *Buckingham* had the advantage of him in *England* (although the King did now hate *Buckingham*, yet was so awed that he durst not discover it.) Then *Buckingham* had all interest in his successor by this journy, so that he laid a present and future foundation of his succeeding greatness.

For all his power and greatness, *Bristol* did not forbear to put all scorns, affronts, and tricks on him, and *Buckingham* lay so open, as gave the other advantage enough by his lascivious carriage and miscarriage. Amongst all his tricks, he plays one so cunningly, that it cost him all the hair on his head, and put him to the dyet; for it should seem he made court to *Conde Olivons* L. a very handsome Lady; But it was so plotted betwixt the Lady, her Husband, and *Bristol*, that instead of that beauty, he had a notorious Stew sent him, and surely his carriage there was so lascivious, that had ever the match been really intended for our Prince, yet such a Companion, or Guardian, was enough to have made them believe he had been that way addicted, and so have frustrated the marriage, that being a grave and sober Nation, *Buckingham* of a light and loose behavior; and had the Prince himself been of an extraordinary well staid temper, the other had been a very ill Guardian unto him.

But now many Lords flockt over, and many Servants, that he might appear the Prince of *England*, and like himself, though he came thither like a private person, many Treaties were, sometimes hope, sometimes dispair, sometimes great assurance, then all dasht again, and however, his entertainment was as great as possible that State could afford; yet was his addresses to, and with the Lady such, as rendred him mean, and a private person, rather than a Prince of that State, that formerly had made *Spain* feel the weight of their anger, and power; and was like a Servant, not a Suiter, for he never was admitted, but to stand bare head in her presence, nor to talk with her, but in a full audience with much company.

At last, after many heats and cools, many hopes and dispairs, the Prince wrote a letter to his Father of a desperate dispair, not only of not injoying his Lady, but of never more returning, with this passage, You must now Sir look upon my Sister and her children, forgetting ever you had such a Son, and never thinking more of me.

Now the folly of this voyage, plotted only by green heads, began to appear, many shewing much sorrow, many smiling at their follies (and in truth glad in their Hearts) and however the King was a cunning dissembler, and shewed much outward sorrow, as he did for Prince *Henries* death, yet something was discerned, which made his Court believe little grief came near his heart, for that hatred he bare to *Buckingham* long (as being satiated with him) and his adoring the rising sun, not looking after the sun setting, made the world believe he would think it no ill bargain to loose his son, so *Buckingham* might be lost also, for had he not been weary of *Buckingham*, he would never have adventured him in such a journey, all his Courtiers knew that very well.

And for a further illustration of his weariness of *Buckingham*, it appeared in the Parliament before, when the King gave so much way to his ruine, that *Buckingham* challenged him that he did seek his ruine, and being generally held a lost man, the King to make it appear it was not so, and that the King durst not avow his own act, brought him off from that Parliament, but *Buckingham* hated the King ever afterwards.

The reason the King so hated *Buckingham* was, (besides his being weary of him and his marriage, after which the Kings edge was ever taken off from all Favorites; yet this had so much the over-awing power of him, that he durst not make shew to affect any other; there was one *Juniossa* a Spanish Embassador extraordinary here, being an old Soldier, and a gallant fellow, thought that *Buckingham* did not give that respect to him, was due to his own person, or to the person of so great a King, whose person he represented; *Juniossa* did as much scorn and slight *Buckingham*, and the Prince, who he found wholly governed by *Buckingham*; for now *Buckingham* had found by many passages, the Kings desire to be rid of him, he made Court to the Prince, and so wrought himself into his affection, that *Damon* and *Pythias* were not more dear to each other, which by no means could the old King away with, nor in truth did any other like or approve of the Prince his poor spirit; fearing it foretold his future inclination, that could ever indure any familiarity with such an one as had put such foul scorn and affronts on him in his time of greatness, with the Father especially, calling to mind the bravery of his brother, who hated the whole Family for their general baseness, although none of them had ever offended him in particular, as this man had done the Prince at two several times, before an infinite concourse, by bidding him in plain terms kiss his arse once, a second time offering to strike him, saying in most undutiful terms, *by God it shall not be so, nor you shall not have it*, lifting up his hand over his head with a Ballon brasser; that the Prince said, what my Lord I *think you intend to strike me:* The first of these at *Roiston*, the second at *Greenwich*. These affronts were not to be indured by a person, but by a prince from a private person, surely it shewed a much less spirit then should have been inherent to a Prince, and after this, to be so dear with him, as to be governed by him all his life time, more than his Father was in the prime of his affection, I can give it no title mean enough; it had been worthy the noble mind of a Prince to have forgotten such injuries, as never to have revenged them when he had been King, but never to have suffered him to have come near his Court, to upbraid him with the sight of so much scorn, and that publickly offered him before: But at that time I well remember some Criticks in Court did not stick to read his future destiny.

This *Juniossa* being a brave daring Gentleman, used some speeches in the derogation of the Prince, and *Buckingham*, as if they were dangerous to the old King; nay, *Juniossa* sent one *Padro Mecestria*, a *Spanish* Jesuite, and a great Statesman, to King *James*, to let him know, that he, under confession, had found the King was by *Buckingham*, or by his procurement, to be killed, but whether by Poyson, Pistol, Dagger, &c. that he could not tell.

The King, after the hearing of this, was extream melancholly, and in that passion was found by *Buckingham* at his return to him. The King, as soon as ever he espied him, said, Ah *Stenny*, *Stenny*, for so he ever called him in familiarity, wilt thou kill me? at which *Buckingham* started, and said, who Sir hath so abused you? at which the King sate silent; out went *Buckingham*, fretting and fuming, asked who had been with the King in his absence? It was told him *Padro Macestria*, then who brought him to the King? it was replyed, the Earl of *Kelly*; then flew *Buckingham* on him, to know how he durst bring any one in to the King in his absence, or without his licence? *Kelly* stood up close to him (for you must know, *Kelly* was the truest alarum to give warning of the downfal of a Favorite, of any in the Court) and knew his power could do him no hurt with the King, in present; although it utterly cast him out of all favor from the King in future.

Then *Buckingham* questioned *Padro Macestria*, which quarrel, *Juniossa* undertook, and told him he would maintain him a Traytor, and wear his Masters person on him; he was a Chivalier, and better born than himself, and would make it good of him with his Sword.

The Prince was by *Buckingham* made to write a Letter of complaint to the King of *Spain*, for abusing him and *Buckingham*; but the King of *Spain* returned the Letter in a kind of scorn, to *Juniossa*, not as blaming him, but rather commending him; and *Juniossa* in scorn sent it to the Prince, as if he should say, there is your Letter to wipe———, which is all it is fit for.

Now have you heard what made the King hate *Buckingham*, you shall also hear the reason of *Buckinghams* extreme hatred to the King, which was believed the cause of his so speedy death. *Yelverton*, a very faithful servant to the King, and his Atturney General, and no less affectionate to *Somerset*, being formerly raised by him without any seeking of his, or so much as within his thought, insomuch as to express his love to *Somerset*, he desired to lay down that great place, rather then aggravate, as his place required, against him. This man, as well out of his faithfulness, as affection to *Somerset*, was made choyce of, to work the downfal of *Buckingham*, in which he apparently shewed himself. But *Buckingham*, as I told you before, out of the Kings fear, that durst not maintain his own design, but left his instrument to the mercy of *Buckinghams* tyranny, being once gotten out of this toil, like a chafed Beare, foamed, and bit at all came near him, and amongst them, first fastened on *Yelverton*, put him out his place, and committed him close prisoner to the Tower. *Yelverton* having shewed himself so faithful to his Master, and he again so unfaithful to him, to leave him to undergoe the whole burden of *Buckinghams* fury, did fly out in some passion before *Balfore*, then Lieutenant of the Tower, and *Buckinghams* great creature.

Balfore telling the Duke of some passages in his passion, the Duke one night about 12 o'clock came in a disguise, and with the Lieutenant only, entred *Yelvertons* lodging, *Yelverton* at first sight started, verily believing, he came in that manner to murther him; yet at last recollected himself, and said: My Lord, have you the Kings warrant for this? the Duke said, no; then said *Yelverton*, how dare you enter a close prisoners lodging? it is as much as your life is worth; and assure yourself, Master Lieutenant, the King shall know of this, and you must answer it: My Lord said, I come to you as a friend, though formerly I confess, upon just cause, your mortal enemy; only to ask you but two questions, which if you will resolve me, I vow to be a greater friend now then ever an enemy, and can, and will restore you fourfold: *Yelverton* told him, if they were such as he might, he would.

The first he asked was, What wrong he had ever done him, that he so greedily thirsted after his blood? *Yelverton* replyed, never any, but I was set on by a power that I could not withstand, to do what I did; he asked him, by whom? by the King your Master said he, who hates you more then any man living, which you might well understand, when in his speech to the Parliament, he said, he would not spare any (no not any that were dearest to him, or lay in his bosom) by which he pointed them to you.

Well said *Buckingham*, I see you have dealt like a Friend with me, by many other concurrences, as well as by this; give me your hand, henceforth you are my friend, and I am yours; and will raise you higher, then I have cast you down, which he had made good, had *Yelverton* lived to have injoyed it, for he was instantly released, and the next preferment a Judges place, and had been Lord Keeper, had not death prevented. And if there were no reason, but his change, from a mortal enemy to so firm a friend, it were sufficient to confirm the truth of this story. But the Author had this from *Yelvertons* own relation, and cannot commend *Yelverton*, because it is verily believed this hastened the Kings death.

Now have you heard the true causes of *Buckinghams* hatred to the King, and the Kings to *Buckingham*, the King having the more power to revenge, had the less courage; *Buckingham* less power, but more courage, sharpened with revenge: And however the world did believe the Kings inclination was out of a religious ground, that he might not revenge, yet it was no other cowardly disposition that durst not adventure; but although the King lost his opportunity on *Buckingham*, yet the black plaister and powder did shew *Buckingham* lost not his on the King; and that it was no fiction but a reallity, that *Padro Macestria* had formerly told the King.

And now to return from this digression, which is not impertinent besides a great secret, (the Prince returns from *Spain*, contrary to expectation) in which the wisdom and gravity of the *Spaniard* failed him, especially if they did believe *Padro Macestria* (besides nature could not long support the old King) and then the *Spaniard* might have made no little advantage by injoying such a pledge: but they have confessed their error, yet do paliate it with having the Prince his faith and his proxy left with *Digby*, and got thence with the very same trick Sir *Francis Michael* said he got out of the Inquisition at *Rome*.

Now is all the fault laid on *Digbyes* false play and unfaithfulness to his Master, and combyning with the *Spaniard*, and by this piece of service expressing his hatred to the *Spaniard* for his own ends (the Subjects of *England* having ever naturally hated them) *Buckingham* from a most hated man then living, from an accused man in the former Parliament, came to be the very darling of this Parliament, and a favorite to the whole Kingdom, which after King *James* his death he as soon lost again, (so inconstant are the multitude.)

In the Banquetting-house before both Houses of Parliament, is *Buckingham* to give an account of his voyage, which he did at large, and to every full point as a further attestation, he saith, how say you Sir? to which the Prince answered *I, yea,* or *yes,* and through all his discourse labored to make *Bristol* as hateful to this Parliament, as himself had been to the former, which, had these things delivered by him, and attested by the Prince, been truths, he had justly deserved death, the accusations were foul and little less then treason, without any legislative power.

Digby had some friends who instantly sent this Declaration into *Spain*, *Digby* acquaints that King, takes his leave of him for *England:* that King sets his danger before him, offers if he will stay with him, seeing it is for his sake, he is likely to suffer, he would make him much greater in honour and fortune then his Master can do, *Digby* gives him thanks, but says, he served so just a Master that would not condemn him unheard, and should he, yet he had much rather suffer under innocency, then lie under the imputation of a false accusation, of a fugitive, and Traytor, for the highest preferment in the world.

Away therefore comes he, puts himself into a desperate passage, least the Parliament should have been dissolved before his coming, and so no place or means left him for his defence, but must lye under those false calumnies, and was here (as the Prince came into *Spain*) sooner then either looked for or welcome.

Into the Parliament comes he, with his hat full of papers, where he puts himself upon this point, that if there were one syllable true that *Buckingham* had delivered, if this (holding up a paper in his hand) be a true copy; I will yield myself guilty of all treasons can be laid to my charge, and said, these papers, (pointing to his hat,) shall make it manifest: Beside some of them shall make *Buckingham* appear a very monster in his lascivious carriages, too unchaste for the ears of this Honorable Assembly; *Bristol* was instantly committed close prisoner to the Tower for a contempt; the next day he was riding through Cheapside in his Coach, by which it appears *Buckinghams* power was in the wain with his old Master, his relation and accusation being scandalous and false; nor durst he bring *Bristol* to any further tryal.

Whether this wound was deeper given by *Bristol*, to *Buckingham*, or the Prince, I will leave to the reader to judge, and will not myself determine; and how *Bristol* hath since stood in favour with the Prince since he was King, may give a conjecture, that he took it as a wound to himself; I am sure it was an ill omen, and hath since given him less credit with his subjects.

And in this Parliament doth *Buckingham* by his under-hand Ministers and Agents, accuse *Cranfield* the Lord Treasurer, in which the Prince also shews himself: *Cranfield* was so hated a fellow for his insolency, that a small accusations would serve the turn, as this truly was, had his care of expending the Kings Treasure been out of true zeal, for it should seem that the Prince sending for monys, *Cranfield* restrained his expence, using some words, that the journey itself was foolishly undertaken, and now must be maintained by prodigality, in which the Revenue of the Kingdom would not satisfie their vast expences; if this had been spoken out of a noble mind, or out of that feeling he had of the Kingdoms misery as being Treasurer he ought to have done had he fallen, it had been with honor and a general compassion, but being spoken out of the pride and insolence of his own heart, whose mind was ever so base, as never to discern what Honor was, nor ever had he any other inherent Honor then what in his Apprenticeship he raked out of the Kennel; besides it was known to be out of hatred, that he was not of councel in the undertaking, he then looking at himself as the only Statesman of all the Councel: He fell without pitty, and with much scorn, as I formerly set down; yet left in an higher estate and better condition then so worthless a fellow, and base Projector deserved, yet afterwards he was again questioned upon his accounts: but all this was nothing, himself and his posterity being left Peers of the Realm.

In this case was the Prince a principal actor, and did duly keep the earliest hours to sit in that Parliament, where, then he descerned so much jugling even to serve his own ends on *Cranfield*, that it was not much to be wondered at, being come to be King, he did not affect them: and it was not so well that a Prince should show so much spleen, though *Cranfield* deserved any ill could be cast on him, and who knows whether God doth now punish by Tallion, to call his own sin to remembrance, and to repent.

In this place I hold it not unfit to shew the Reader how the King hath ever been abused, and would be abused, by over much credulity in the treaty of *Spain* for marriages, as well as in all other Negotiations.

You shall now perceive how the King was abused in this treaty, which was an error inexcusable, in himself and whole Councel. The *Italians* having a Proverb, ' He that deceives me once, its his fault; but if twice, its my fault:' this second time therefore could not but be the only fault of the King and Councel.

In Prince *Henry* his life time, the King had a little man, but a very great and wise Counsellor, his Secretary of State, little *Salisbury*, that great Statesman, who did inherit all his Fathers wisdom, as well as his Offices, and the same came little short of the father, who was held the greatest Statesman in the world, of his time. It is true, that one State may abuse another, but not find out the abuse is an unpardonable fault in any Statesman.

There was a treaty in the like case for Prince *Henry*, *Salisbury* instantly discovered the jugling before any other did think of any, for although it went forward cunningly, yet did *Salisbury* so put the Duke of *Lerma* unto it, that either it must be so, or they must confess their jugling.

The Duke of *Lerma* denyed that everthere had been any treaty, or any intention from that State; *Salisbury* sent for the Embassador to a full Councel, told him how he had abused the King and State, about a treaty for Marriage, which he had no Commission for; that therefore he was lyable to the laws of our Kingdom; for when any Embassador doth abuse a State by their Mrs. Commission, then the servant was freed; but without Commission, was culpable and lyable to be punished by the Laws of that State, as being disavowed to be served to the King his Master; the Ambassador answered gravely, he did not understand the cause of his coming, therefore was then unprepared to give any answer, but on Monday he would again come, this being Saturday, and give his answer. On Monday he comes, begins with these words, ' My soul is my Gods, my life my Masters, my reputation my own, I will not forfeit the first and last, to preserve the second;' then layes down his Commission, and Letters of instruction, under the Treasurers own hand, he acquitted himself honestly to this State, yet lost his own, being instantly sent for home, where he lived and dyed in disgrace, here was *Legatus vir bonus peregre missus sed non admentiendum, reipublicæ causa:* and had we had as honest and good Statesmen in aftertimes, this State could not have been abused in all Treaties.

By this you see the advantage and benefit of one wise Counsellor in a whole State; and although *Solomon* says, By the multitude of Counsel doth the Kingdom florish, yet surely he intended they should be wise men that are Counsellors; for we had such a multitude of Counsellors, that a longer table, and a larger Counsel-chamber was provided, yet our State was so far from florishing, that it had been almost utterly destroyed; this was the last Statesman worthy of that name; and now are the ancient stock of Statesmen decayed, and with them all our honour and glory.

I shall now bring my story to an end, as I shall this Kings life; although I have made some digressions, yet all pertinent to the discourse of this Kings reign.

He now goes to his last hunting journey, I mean the last of the year, as well as of his life, which he ever ended in Lent, and was seized on by an ordinary Tertian Ague, which at the season, according to the Proverb, was Physio for the King, but it proved not so to him; and poor King, what was but Physick to any other, was made mortal to him: yet not the Ague, as himself confessed to a servant of his, who cryed courage, Sir, this is but a small fit, the next will be none at all, at which he most earnestly looked; and said, Ah, it is not the Ague afflicteth me, but the black plaister and powder given me, and laid to my stomack; and in truth, the plaister so tormented him, that he was glad to have it pulled off, and with it the skin also; nor was it fair dealing, if he had fair play (which himself suspected) often saying to *Montgomery*, whom he trusted above all men, in his sickness, for Gods sake, look I have fair play to bring in an Emprick, to apply any Medicines, whilst those Physicians appointed to attend him, were at dinner; nor could any but *Buckingham* answer it with less than his life at that present, as he had the next Parliament had it not been dissolved upon the very questioning him for the Kings death, and all those that prosecuted him, utterly disgraced and banished the Court.

Buckingham coming into the Kings Chamber, even when he was at the point of death, and an honest servant of the Kings crying: Ah my Lord, you have undone us, all his poor servants, although you are so well provided you need not care: at which *Buckingham* kickt at him, who caught his foot, and made his head first come to ground, where *Buckingham* presently rising, run to the dying Kings bed side, and cryed, Justice, Sir, I am abused by your servant, at which the poor King mournfully fixed his eyes on him, as who would have said (not wrongfully) yet without speech or sence.

It were worth the knowledge, what his confession was, or what other expressions he made of himself, or any other; but that is only known to the dead Arch-Bishop *Abbot*, and the living Bishop *Williams*, then Lord Keeper, and it was thought that *Williams* had blabbed something which incensed the Kings anger, and *Buckinghams* hatred so much against him, that the loss of his place could not be expiatory sufficient, but his utter ruin must be determined, and that not upon any known crime, but upon circumstances, and Examinations, to pick out faults, committed in his whole life time; but his greatest crime for the present, (no question) was *lapsus linguæ*, but *quod defertur non aufertur*, for although he escaped by the calm of this Parliament, yet is he more ruined by this Parliament, and his own folly; and truly we may observe the first Judgment of God on him, for flying from the Parliament his protector, to give wicked Counsel to the King, his former prosecutor.

And now have I brought this great Kings Reign to an end, in a volant discourse, and shall give you his Character in brief, and so leave him in peace after his life, who was stiled the King of peace in his life.

THE CHARACTER OF KING JAMES.

THIS Kings Character is much easier to take then his Picture, for he could never be brought to sit for the taking of that, which is the reason of so few good pieces of him; but his Character was obvious to every eye.

He was of a middle stature, more corpulent through his cloathes then in his body, yet fat enough, his cloathes ever being made large and easie, the Doublets quilted for steletto proof, his Breeches in plates, and full stuffed: He was naturally of a timorous disposition, which was the reason of his quilted doublets, his eye large, ever rowling after any stranger came in his presence, in so much, who that for shame have left the room, as being out of countenance; his Beard was very thin; his tongue too large for his mouth, which ever made him drink very uncomely, as if eating his drink, which came out into the cup of each side his mouth; his skin was as soft as Taffeta Sarsnet, which felt so, because he never washt his hands, only rub'd his fingers ends slightly, with the wet-end of a Napkin, his legs were very weak, having as was thought some foul play in his youth, or rather before he was born, that he was not able to stand at seven years of age, that weakness made him ever leaning on other mens shoulders; his walk was ever circular, his fingers ever in that walk fidling about his cod-piece; he was very intemperate in his drinking; however in his old age, and *Buckinghams* jovial Suppers, when he had any turn to do with him, made him sometimes over-taken, which he would the very next day remember, and repent with tears. It is true that he drank very often, which was rather out of a custom than any delight, and his drinks were of that kind of strength, as Frontiniack, Canary, High Canary wine, Tent wine, and *Scotish* Ale, that had he not had a very strong brain, might have daily been overtaken, although he seldom drank at any one time above four spoonfulls, many times not above one or two; he was very constant in all things, his Favorites excepted, in which he loved change, yet he never cast down any he once raised from the height of greatness, though from their wanted nearness, and privacy; unless by their own default, by opposing his change, as in *Somersets* case: yet had he not been in that foul poysoning business, and so cast down himself; I do verily believe not him neither; for all his other Favorites he left great in Honor, great in Fortune; and did much love *Mountgomery*, and trusted him more at the very last gasp, then at the first minute of his Favoriteship: in his Dyet, Apparel, and Journeys, was very constant; in his Apparel so constant, as by his good will he would never change his cloathes till very ragges; his fashion never: insomuch as one bringing to him a Hat of a *Spanish* Block, he cast it from him, swearing he neither loved them nor their fashions. Another time, bringing him Roses on his Shoes, asked, if they would make him a ruff-footed-Dove? one yard of six penny Ribbond served that turn; his Dyet and Journeys were so constant, that the best observing Courtier of our time was wont to say, was he asleep seven years, and then awakened, he would tell where the King every day had been, and every dish he had had at his Table.

He was not very uxorious, though he had a very brave Queen that never crossed his designs, nor intermedled with State affaires, but ever complyed with him, against the nature of any; but of a mild spirit in the change of Favorites; for he was ever best, when furthest from the Queen, and that was thought to be the first grounds of his often removes which afterwards proved habitual. He was unfortunate in the marriage of his Daughter, and so was all Christendom besides, but sure the Daughter was more unfortunate in a Father then he in a Daughter; he naturally loved not the sight of a Soldier, nor of any valiant man; and it was an observation that Sir *Robert Mansell* was the only valiant man he ever loved, and him he loved so intirely, that for all *Buckinghams* greatness with the King, and his hatred of Sir *Robert Mansell*, yet could not that alienate the Kings affections from him; insomuch as when by the instigation of *Cottington* then Embassador in *Spain*; by *Buckinghams* procurement, the *Spanish* Embassador came with a great complaint against Sir *Robert Mansell*, then at *Argiers*, to suppress the Pirates. That he did support him having never a friend there (though many) that durst speak in his defence, the King himself defended him in these words: " My Lord Embassador, I cannot believe this, for I made choice myself of him, out of those reasons; I know him to be valiant, honest, and Nobly descended as most in my Kingdom, and will never believe a man thus qualified will do so base an act." He naturally loved honest men, that were not over active, yet never loved any man heartily until he had bound him unto him by giving him some suite, which he thought bound the others love to him again; but that argued a poor disposition in him, to believe that any thing but a Noble mind, seasoned with virtue, could make any firm love or union, for mercinary minds are carryed away with a greater prize, but noble minds alienated with nothing but publick disgraces.

He was very witty, and had as many witty jests as any man living at which he would not smile himself, but deliver them in a grave and serious manner. He was very liberal, of what he had not in his own gripe, and would rather part with 100*l*. he never had in his keeping, then one twenty shilling piece within his own custody: He spent much, and had much use of his subjects purses, which bred some clashing with them in Parliament, yet would always come off, and end with a sweet and plausible close; and truly his bounty was not discommendable, for his raising Favorites was the worst: Rewarding old servants, and relieving his Native Country-men, was infinitely more to be commended in him, then condemned. In sending Embassadors, which were no less chargeable then dishonourable and unprofitable to him and his whole Kingdom; for he was ever abused in all negotiations, yet he had rather spend 100,000*l*. on Embassies, to keep or procure peace with dishonour, then 10,000*l*. on an Army that would have forced peace with honour: He loved good laws, and many made in his time, and in his last Parlament for the good of his Subjects, and suppressing Promoters, and progging fellows, gave way to that *Nullum tempus*, &c. to be confined for sixty years, which was more beneficial to the Subjects in respect of their quiets, then all the Parliaments had given him during his whole Reign. By his frequenting Sermons he appeared Religious; yet his Tuesday Sermons if you will believe his own Countrymen, that lived in those times when they were erected, and well understood the cause of erecting them were dedicated for a strange piece of devotion.

He would make a great deal too bold with God in his passion, both in cursing and swearing, and one strain higher, verging on blasphemy; But would in his better temper say, he hoped God would not impute them as sins, and lay them to his charge, seeing they proceeded from passion: He had need of great assurance, rather than hopes, that would make dayly so bold with God.

He was so crafty and cunning in petty things, as the circumventing any great man, the change of a Favorite, insomuch as a very wise man was wont to say, he believed him the wisest fool in Christendome, meaning him wise in small things, but a fool in weighty affaires.

He ever desired to prefer mean men in great places, that when he turned them out again, they should have no friend to bandy with them: And besides, they were so hated by being raised from a mean estate, to over-top all men, that every one held it a pretty recreation to have them often turned out. There was in this Kings time, at one instant living, two Treasurers, three Secretaries, two Lord Keepers, two Admirals, three Lord Chief Justices, yet but one in play, therefore this King had a pretty faculty in putting out and in: By this you may perceive in what his wisdom consisted, but in great and weighty affairs, even at his wits end.

He had a trick to cousen himself with bargains under hand, by taking 1000*l.* or 10,000*l.* as a bribe, when his Counsel was treating with his Customers to raise them to so much more yearly, this went into his Privy purse; wherein he thought he had over-reached the Lords, but cousened himself; but would as easily break the bargain upon the next offer, saying, he was mistaken and deceived, and therefore no reason he should keep the bargain; this was often the case with the Farmers of the Customes; He was infinitely inclined to prayer, but more out of fear then conscience, and this was the greatest blemish this King had through all his Reign, otherwise he might have been ranked with the very best of our Kings, yet sometimes would he shew pretty flashes which might easily be discerned to be forced, not natural; And being forced, could have wished, rather, it would have recoiled back to himself, then carryed to that King it had concerned, least he might have been put to the tryal, to maintain his seeming valor.

In a word, take him altogether and not in pieces, such a King I wish this Kingdom have never any worse, on the condition, not any better; for he lived in peace, dyed in peace, and left all his Kingdoms in a peaceable condition, with his own Motto:

Beati Pacifica.

NOW having brought this peaceable King to rest in all peace, the 27th of *March*, his son, by the sound of the Trumpet, was Proclaimed King, by the name of CHARLES the FIRST.

His Fathers Reign began with a great plague, and we have seen what his Reign was; His Sons with a greater plague, and the greatest that was ever in these parts, we shall see what his Reign will be, and the effects of this plagues end, hang as a fatal commet over this Kingdom, in some parts, and over *London* in more particular, ever since: and we earnestly pray we may not fall into the hands of men, but under the reproofs of our merciful God.

This king was not Crowned with that solemnity, all other Kings have formally been, by riding through the City in all state, although the same Triumphes were provided for him, as sumptuous as for any other; this, some have taken as an ill omen: Its further reported, which I will not believe, that he took not the usual Oath all Kings are bound unto, at their Coronation, and its to be read in *Covells* book, if so, sure its a worse omen:

One more observation is, of this King, which I remember not in any other Kingdom, I am confident never in this; That with this King did also rise his Fathers Favorite, and in much more glory and luster than in his Father time, as if he were an inheritor of his Sons favors, as the Son of the Fathers Crown, and this as it happened was the worst omen of all, for whereas in the Fathers time, there was some kind of moderation, by reason he was weary of the insolency of his Favorite; in the sons time he reigned like an impetuous storm, treading down all before him that stood in his way, and would not yield to him or comply with him; This shewed no Heroical or Kingly spirit, for the King ever to endure him, that had put such scorns, and insolent affronts on him in his fathers time.

This King (as his Father did set in peace) did rise like a *Mars*, as if he would say, *Arma virumq; Cano*, and to that end to make himself more formidable to *Spain* and *France*, he called a Parliament, wherein never subjects expressed more hearty affections to a Prince; and in truth, were more loving than wise, for as if for an income to welcome him, they gave him two intire Subsidies, and in it brake the very foundation and privileges of Parliament, which never was wont to give Subsidies but as a thankful gratuity for enacting good Lawes, therefore it is but Gods justice to repay them with Tallions lawes, to have their Privileges broken, seeing they first chalked out the way; the King in requital of this great love of theirs, did instantly dissolve the Parliament, which hath bred such ill blood in the veines of the Subjects to their Soveraign, and the Sovereign to the Subject, that its like to produce an epidemical infection.

But the occasion taken to dissolve it was worst of all, for *Buckingham* by his insolent behaviour had not only lost that love, his hatred to *Spaine* had procured him, but was now grown into such an hatred that they fell on him for the death of his old Master, which had been of long time whispered; the Examinations bred such confessions, that it looked with an ugly deformed poysonous countenance, and nothing but the dissolution of that Parliament could have saved his dissolution, and that with a brand of shame and infamy, as well as ingratitude.

I remember I heard an old Parliament man, and a noble Gentleman of that Committee for Examinations say, at first he derided the very thought of it; but after the first dayes Examination it proved so foul, as that he both hated and scorned the name of *Buckingham*; and though man would not punish it, God would, which proved an unhappy prediction.

This dissolving the Parliament was ill relished by the people, and the seeming cause worse, and to make the case worse, and that it most needst needs be the evident cause; *Buckinghams* Counsels were so stupid and himself so insolent, that he did think it a glory to disgrace all that followed that business, that Parliament, or seemed inquisitive; and caused many old Servants of the Kings, he formerly favoured very much, to be banished from Court, never to return more, nor did they ever, as *Clare, Crofts*, Sir *F. Stewart*, nay D. *Cray*, his Phisitian, who from his very childhood, had the general repute of a very honest man, for expressing himself like an honest man in the Kings presence, was instantly dismissed, never could recover his place or favor more.

Now also is *Williams* Lord Keeper turned out of his place, and *Coventry* the Kings Atturney (who had *Buckingham* lived, had as soon) followed in his stead.

Then goes *Buckingham* unto *France* on a stately Embassie for the Lady the King had seen, and set an affection on in his passage to *Spaine*, which was obtained with small intreaty.

CONCLUDING REMARKS.

Now doth *Buckingham* soare so high in his Masters favours and pride of his own heart, as he alters all great Officers, makes war against *France* and *Spaine*, the quarrel only his, voiced to be on strange grounds, the success accordingly. Navies, Armies, and nothing but war appears, as if we intended in time to conquer all that opposed; L. *Wimbledon* the General, from whom as little was expected, as he performed, carrying a powerful Army to *Cales*, after an infinite expence and drinking much *Spanish* Wines, and beating out the heads of what they could not drink, returned as like a valiant Commander, as he then was reputed.

Then is Denbigh sent into France to aide Rochille, who managed it better then his great Kinsman, who would afterwards needs go to do great exploits, for he brought his ship and men safe again, the other left his men in powdering tubs, as if he meant to have them kept sweet against his comming thether : In short, this unhappy voyage lost all the honor our glorious ancestors have ever gotten over that Nation, there being so many brave gentlemen wilfully lost, as if that voyage had been on purpose plotted to disable our Nation, by taking away so many gallant brave young spirits.

FINIS.

INDEX.

Abbott, Archbishop, 25, 54.
Achmoty, John, 19.
Algice, Earl of, 42.
Anne, (James's Queen), 12.
Annundale, Earl of, 19, 37.
Armstrong, Archer, the Jester, 29.
Arundel, Earl of, 5.
Aremberg, Count of, 8, 11.
Aston, Sir Roger, 2, 4, 28.
Aston, Sir Walter, 45.
Ashley, Sir Anthony, 42.
Bacon, Lord, 39, 41, 43, 44.
Balfore, 49.
Balmerino, Earl, 5.
Bath, 4.
Bailey, James, 19.
Binden, 30.
Brussells, 29.
Bruce, the Astrologer, 26.
Brook, George, 10, 12.
Bristol, Earl of, 10, 44, 45, 50.
Buchanan, 22.
Buckhurst, Lord, 5.
Bullion, Duke of, 4.
Buckingham, Duke of, 40, 41, 42, 43, 44, 46, 47, 48, 49, 50, 54, 56, 58, 61.
Car, Mr. Robert, 19.
Car, Sir Robert, 20.
Carlisle, Earl of, 7, 19.
Carew, Sir George, 13.
Carew, Sir Robert, 1, 6.
Castile, Constable of, 8, 9.
Calais, 8.
Cæsar, Julius, 11.
Cæsar, Sir Julius, 13, 42.
Cecil, Sir Robert, 4.
Charlton, 30.
Charing Cross, 20.
Charles I. 59.
Coventry, Attorney, 60.
Coke, Sir Edward, Chief Justice, 31, 34, 35, 36, 38.
Cottington, Francis Lord, 44, 57.
Copenger, 21.
Cobham, Lord, 6, 10, 11, 12, 13.
Cranfield, Earl of Middlesex, 27, 28, 36, 38, 44, 51.

Cranborn, 30.
Clark, the Papist, 10, 11.
Davenant, Bishop, 41.
Denny, Lord, 6.
Dingwell, Lord, 20.
Drake, Sir F. 14.
Dromon, David, (the Jester), 29.
Dunbar, Earl of, 5, 18, 19.
Egerton, Lord Keeper, 5, 39, 43.
Elizabeth, Queen, 1, 2, 6, 17, 26, 34.
Elizabeth, Princess, (Daughter of James I.) 4, 31.
Elizabeth, Queen of Bohemia, 31.
Elfeston, Secretary, 5.
Elwaies, Sir J. 22, 23, 29, 38.
Essex, Earl of, 4, 10, 13.
Essex, Second Earl of, 21.
Essex, Countess, 25, 35.
Essex-house, 6.
Fines, Mistress, 25.
Finit, Sir John, 28, 29.
Flood, Dr. 35.
Fotherby, Bishop of Sarum, 40.
Forman, Simon, 34.
Franklyn, 23, 30, 35, 38.
Gib, John, 19.
Goring, Sir George, 28, 29.
Gowrie, (the Conspirator), 3.
Grey, Lord de Wilton, 6, 10, 11, 12.
Graveling, 8.
Greenwich, 36, 47.
Guildhall, London, 36.
Hay, Mr. James, 6.
Hatton, Lord, 30.
Hampton-Court, 31.
Hartford, Earl of, 13, 14, 15.
Hatfield, 26.
Henry, Prince, 26, 46, 52.
Hewme, Sir George, 3, 4.
Heath, Attorney, 40.
Holland, 34.
Howard, Sir Thomas, 30.
Holdernesse, Earl of, 3.
Helens Church, (St.) 13 n.
Ingram, Cofferer of the Household, 38, 27.
James I. 2, 16, 17, 18, 26, 29, 34, 36, 42, 44, 50.

INDEX.

Juniossa, (Embassador), 47, 48.
Kelly, Earl of, 18, 27, 48.
Kinlosse, Lord, 6.
Lake, (Clerk of the Signet), 17, 18.
Lambeth, 34, 35.
Lennox, Duke of, 13.
Levison, Sir Richard, 14.
Lerma, Duke of, 53.
Loveston, John, 36, 37.
Loreskeine, Lord, 36.
London, 4, 6, 7, 32, 35.
Lindley, Bernard, 19.
Ludworth, 30.
Mansel, Sir Robert, 7, 8, 9, 14, 15, 39, 56, 57.
May, Sir Humfrey, 30, 36.
May, Herrick, 36.
Marshall, Sir George, 36.
Margrave, Dean, 40.
Madrid, 14, 15.
Mecestria, Pedro, 48, 49.
Michael, Sir Francis, 50.
Millisert, Sir John, 29.
Monson, Sir Thomas, 15, 16, 32, 33, 35, 36.
Moore, Sir George, 36, 37, 38.
Morby, a wood-cutter, 43.
Montgomery, Earl of, 19, 54, 56.
Murrey, Gideon, 19.
Muscovia, 6.
Neale, Bishop of Rochester, 24, 25.
Newmarket, 16.
Norfolk, Thomas, fourth Duke of, 5.
Northampton, Earl of, 5, 7, 8, 18, 21, 27.
Olivons, Conde, 46.
Overbury, Sir Thomas, 20, 21, 22, 23, 24, 29, 30, 34, 35, 38.
Parham, Mr. 10, 12.
Palsgrave, Elector of, 26.
Perkins, Sir Christopher, 42.
Pembroke, Earl of, 9, 33.
Purbeck, 31, 43.
Puddle Dock, 35.
Ramsay, Sir John, 3.
Raleigh, Sir W. 6, 10, 11, 12.
Reeve, Mr. 29.
Richmond, 1.

Roney, Duke of Sully, 8.
Royston, (Town of), 16, 31, 32, 33, 47.
Rochester, Viscount, 21.
Salisbury, Earl of, 5, 6, 8, 10, 11, 13, 16, 18, 19, 20, 26, 52.
Scots, Mary, Queen of, 5.
Shrewsbury, Countess of, 29.
Sherborne Castle, 10.
Somerset, Earl of, 22, 25, 27, 28, 29, 30, 31, 32, 35, 36, 37, 38, 44, 48, 49, 56.
Souch, Sir Edward, 28.
Solomon, King, 53.
Southampton, Lord, 13.
Spain, King of, 48.
Stewart, Sir F. 60.
Suffolk, Earl of, 5, 13, 18, 20, 21, 27, 44.
Suffolk, Countess of, 9, 20.
Suffolk-house, 7.
Symes, 33.
Theobalds, 16, 17, 31.
Thames, (River), 35.
Thrumbels, the Agent, 29, 30.
Turner, Sir Jerome, 8.
Turner, Mrs. 30, 33, 34, 38.
Villers, Mr. George, 28, 38.
Villers, Sir George, 30, 31.
Watson, the Papist, 10, 11, 12.
Wade, Lieutenant, 11, 13.
Walsingham, Secretary, 17.
Walden, Lord, 30.
Wanstead Park, 38.
Weston, 22, 23, 24, 29, 30, 33, 34, 38.
Westminster, 34.
Weston, Rev. Mr. 41.
Whitehall, 31, 42.
Wilton, Wilts, 9.
Winchester, 11.
Winchester, Bishop of, 24.
Windsor, 13, 31, 41.
Willoughby, Dr. 35 n.
Williams, Bishop, 43, 44, 54, 60.
Wimbledon, Lord, 61.
Worcester, Earl of, 5, 8, 13, 18.
Yelverton, 48, 49.
York, 3, 4.

CPSIA information can be obtained at www.ICGtesting.com
Printed in the USA
BVOW02s2150011214

377515BV00007B/34/P